DAVID LANGDOWN

Bubbles

Blood, Sweat and Beers

Editing, design, typesetting and publishing by UK Book Publishing
UK Book Publishing
www.ukbookpublishing.com
ISBN: 978-1-914195-41-9

Foreword

This is a book, which will hopefully give a small insight to the life in the bar trade.

Some of the do's and don'ts, but primarily about my own personal experiences.

The characters who I have met along the way. Some situations I have found myself in.

People and events that have happened during my time in the trade and before I came into the trade.

Over the period of twenty-two and a half years, almost our best working years of work, what I have witnessed and the turmoil, which I have experienced, with some blood, sweat and a few beers to go with it along the way.

One of the reasons for me to write this book is because, first of all, it is a non-fiction book–all of this actually happened. Another reason is probably because I feel that 'Bubbles' has a special place in my heart and many a time since I have left, people still come to me and ask about things or events that had happened there. I suppose it could be because of where we are in our lives right now and the years of growing up, most of them were during 'Bubbles' years or even spending our time there during those 'growing up' years.

The town and the people at that time.

I suppose this is a bit of an autobiography, but it also mostly incorporates other people.

Chapter 1
Where it all began

R ewind to March 1985. It was nearing the end of the UK's NCB (National Coal Board) miners' strike, the major industrial action during Thatcher's government to shut down the British coal industry. Life for many hard-working coal miners and their families was hard or, to put it bluntly, pretty shit. This accounted for the vast majority of Ashington people.

I too had endured my own fair share of bad luck, financial turmoil and genuine hardship throughout this time with my dad, Geordie, being a miner on the front line of the strike. The strike lasted a year, beginning in March 1984 and ending the following year in March 1985. When you truly reach the bottom, living a life of near poverty in a first world country, the promise that *the only way is up* really is often the only aspect of hope you clutch onto; praying to God that one day things will get better.

I hoped that those days of betterment would come soon. I can recall every fine detail about the moments which clustered together and aided my world to finally begin to spin once again. I will recount throughout this book the key moments which helped to define the path of my life, but now I speak of one particularly pertinent moment where it really did all begin.

It was Friday 12th April 1985. I nostalgically recall standing in the cellar below two shops which were situated along Ashington's main shopping street. It was the day that the magistrates granted my licence.

I had been working in the cellar for a few months by this point, converting it from a record shop to a wine bar. Wine bars were rapidly becoming a growing trend at the time, offering a somewhat cosmopolitan taste of contemporary life. Permission was granted by the council for the change of use to the building on the condition that an alcohol licence was passed by the police and the magistrates (that's the way it was back then). Looking back, I had done everything the opposite way round by building the bar before having had any licence granted. Prior to the opening of the wine bar, me and my girlfriend Ann ran the cellar as a record shop, but things were tough. I often wondered about the time when the cellar was a folk club years before we ran Cellar Records, realising the building's potential as a live music venue. The cellar had unique potential, situated underground, the acoustics were second to none and the ultimate selling point was, there were no neighbours to complain about noise. I recognised the hardship and times of despair everyone had faced, but realised the gap in the market for any live music and the potential interest this could create in the traditional, working-class town.

Ann and I, my brother Paul and a couple of my friends rallied together to get the bar to a standard before we could finally open

Taking down the sign

the doors to 'Bubbles Wine Bar'–the iconic name that still goes strong to this day was chosen by Ann. Bubbles being a name I argued with her over numerous times with regards to its childish connotations, but I believe that if something becomes a success, the name will follow.

It was now 5.00pm on Saturday 13th April 1985. I was putting on the last piece of wallpaper, thinking to myself that I had to go home and get washed and changed, then to be back in the bar for 6.00pm. I only had a pushbike and lived a couple of miles away.

Off I scurried and got myself freshened up, then back on the pushbike and made my way to Bubbles. I arrived with about five minutes to spare, hurried down the stairs, put on all the lights and had the bar ready to open.

Ann, my brother Paul and a couple of friends, who were to be my new staff, were all there. This is it, time now to open the new bar.

I went upstairs to unlock the door, then returned back downstairs ready for action!

The door opened and in walked my mother and stepdad.

We were all anxious, nervous and excited.

I looked around with dread and despair. All that hard work flashed before my eyes and the regret began to build in my thoughts. An hour went by and in filtered only a handful of customers. I really felt my stomach begin to turn as I thought to myself, "This can't be it!"

Alas, just as I thought it was the beginning of the end, the local rugby team came hurtling through the door and within seconds, the whole place was filling up. You would think a bus had just pulled up outside and everyone was coming in from the bus. What a relief. My luck was miners, who had returned to work and just having received their first pay cheque after the strike.

The whole town was experiencing shared commonalities as it celebrated the end of solace, poignant times and looked forward to the revival of the spirit of Ashington.

Better days had arrived and the whole town embraced its newest member of the pub trade–Bubbles.

Chapter 2
School Days

Years before, around 1967 when I was at junior school, my teacher was Mr Doug Cadwell, he and a couple of other teachers were into folk music. Mr Cadwell on a couple of occasions brought musicians to our school to perform in the hall. I remember The Spinners were a favourite at the time. Mr Cadwell, along with a couple of others, ran the town's folk club. This was called the Lamp Glass Cellar Club, situated believe it or not, at the same place as Bubbles.

I remember one occasion, Mr Cadwell had a guy performing at the folk club in the evening. He was called Don Partridge. This is the chap who was on *Top of the Pops* with a song called *Rosie*. He was called the King of the Buskers. He was a one-man band. Well Doug Cadwell arranged for a couple of my classmates to go and meet Partridge off the bus. They brought him and another guy who was his manager I think, to our classroom. We were all fascinated by this… we had Don Partridge playing for us in our classroom. What a time! The newspapers were there, and some of the lads in the class put on Don's equipment. i.e. bass drum on their back, a harmonic on a bracket around their neck and a huge acoustic guitar. Shortly after his appearance, our school formed a 'Rosie group'. We learned the song *Rosie* and played it in the school hall (I played the cymbals!). This was the start of my love of music.

Chapter 3
Geordie

In 1985 I was living with my father in a small flat in Ashington. My father worked for the National Coal Board; he was a driver. He transported large machinery from one pit to another. Sometimes, the machines were in the local area workshops for repair. I served my apprenticeship at these workshops after leaving school. I was an apprentice welder. I used to occasionally bump into my dad there, whilst he was bringing machines in or collecting them.

My father George, or Geordie as he was known, would frequently visit Bubbles in the early days. He would call in at lunchtime and have some lunch. Then he would call in again most evenings. He was one of the lads.

He followed our tug of war team around, coming to venues. When the lads came in the bar at weekends, he would be there amongst them all. His problem was, he did like a drink and sometimes a bit too much.

Years before Bubbles, there would be many a night, I would be at home and the telephone would ring. A voice at the other end would say "Can I speak with David. We have your father here in

Ashington hospital."

There were many times he would have black eyes or have cut his head and even broken his glasses.

He had fallen down drunk.

I got a call on 13th May 1989 to be exact. My father had been admitted to Ashington hospital again.

When I arrived, I was greeted by nurses who looked a bit sheepish. "Are you George's next of kin?" I was asked, before proceeding to tell me that he had passed away.

I was led into a room where he lay and I walked over and put my hand on his brow. He looked peaceful. "He has had a massive heart attack," one of the nurses told me.

I visited him again in the chapel of rest and once again I went over to him and put my hand on his brow, but this time I got a shiver down my spine. He was cold as ice. That is when the realisation finally hit me.

I took control of things from then on, arranging his funeral with his brothers and sister.

We decided to bury my dad at Saint John's Church in Ashington.

On the day of his funeral, the church was packed. Not everyone could get into the church for the service; some people had to stand outside. What a fantastic send off.

Thank you to everyone who attended that day.

1984-85 was a desperate time. I was in a flat, living with my dad; I had given up the record shop and I was waiting for the change of use for it to be converted into a bar. I was unemployed and my dad was on strike. He would go to the picket lines. When he did this, the union would pay each man £5.00 and they would get bacon sandwiches and a cup of tea for breakfast for free. £5 went a long way then. Geordie was a drinker, and he went to the club religiously. Back then, you could score a pint of beer for just eleven pence, during the strike.

I received my unemployment benefit, paid once every fortnight. From that, I paid the electric and bought food. My girlfriend, Ann, helped with the food a lot of the time as she had a job at the local dentist, training to be a dental nurse. We had a coal fire along with the majority of people in the town in those days, especially the miners who got a coal allowance. But as the pits were closed, there was no coal being delivered. We had no heating and no hot water. I remember the summer of '84. It was a long, hot summer. I remember people commenting on the miners' suntans. But that was soon forgotten about when the winter came. If there was anything made of wood, it got burned. Fences, trees pulled down to burn.

Families were being torn apart. I saw brothers, one working for the NCB on the picket line and the other, working for the police, having to control the picket lines. They were one of the two brothers who stayed together through all of this. My brother Paul worked for the police at the time; he was a trainee wages clerk. There were a few stories about the police making a lot of money and buying properties abroad from this. The police have been an issue throughout my time at Bubbles and I will come to this later.

During the miners' strike of 1984-5, we had a hot summer followed by a very cold winter which seemed to go on forever. Or, maybe, it was just the place I was in at the time. I had closed down the record shop and was waiting to start the work of changing the cellar into a wine bar. Time dragged its heels. It was all red tape—what I mean by this, is that it seemed to take forever for the council to grant permission for the change of use from the record shop to the new wine bar. Trying to juggle this whilst liaising with the breweries to see if I was able to have some money in the form of a grant or loan. It felt that one was waiting for the other, when in reality, it was the normal way in which businesses are managed.

This winter was the worst I have ever experienced, living with my father in a council flat. My dad working for the NCB who were on strike. I heard that some poor miners got their electric disconnected because they had no money to pay for it. Everything that burned was stripped down and put on the open fires in people's homes to keep them warm. I went to the beach on several occasions to see if I could pick up some wood or sea coal. This was a regular sight in those days, where coal was washed up onto the beaches and people would bag it up. Some people made a livelihood from collecting sea coal, putting it into trailers, and get their horses to pull it off the beach. This would be bagged and sold.

Anyway, getting back to my own attempt of collecting sea coal. I had an old bicycle which I would ride down to the beach, approx. 3 miles from our flat. When I got there, the beach was full of people, all with the same idea. Remember, this was the peak of winter, cold, wet and windy. We were all wrapped up in heavy clothes to keep warm. I must have been on the beach for about 4-5 hours only to manage a bag and a half of dross, coal the size of a grain of sand (part of the time, there was just as much sand intermixed with the coal, not ideal for the fire). Soaked to the skin and freezing cold, I ventured home. By this point, those 3 miles felt like 6. Arriving home, at what must have been around 6pm, I noticed my dad who had been out on the picket line all day. He had been fed and watered, he had been home and burnt off what little fuel we had, got himself washed and changed and was away out. Off to the Working Men's club to spend his 5 pounds that he received for picketing.

I then had to scramble twigs and pieces of wood to light a fire and put on this wet dross, which was a ridiculous attempt to start a fire to get warm.

On another occasion, I remember my dad was out on the picket line and we had no food at home. I found a large potato that must have fallen out of a bag at the bottom of a cupboard. 'Chips'... I thought! I hastily chopped the potato into chips. I scraped what loose change I could find in the flat–in those days we were still using half penny coins; I knew the price of a loaf of bread was 24 pence at the supermarket. I scrambled together 24 pence, most of it in half pennies. I ran to the local Co-op store at the top of the street and went to get a loaf of bread, to go with my chips. When I picked it up, to my horror, it was 25 pence. I put it back and scurried around looking to find a smaller loaf, or cheaper alternative. But, to no avail. With my handful of coins, I turned and headed home.

I cooked off the chips, and man were they tasty.

I went for walks to keep warm as we had little or no fuel to burn.

I would walk for miles, look at people's houses with the lights on inside and think to myself, are they a family on strike? Some of the miners had wives and others in the household who were working so it didn't hit them as hard, but taking nothing away from them, I know they felt how difficult it was. The difference was, they had a warm house and food on the table.

I would walk past my mother's house a lot. The curtains were closed, but the lights were on. Boy did it look warm. I never went in, as I had been told to get out in years previous. My mother had married again. Ken, my stepfather. Ken was also on strike as his job was a winder man. This is someone who works at the entrance of the coal mine where the miners would get into a cage and be lowered down underground to work their shifts. My mother worked for the NHS, she was a physio helper at Wansbeck hospital. She was working throughout the strike. There were 3 kids in the house, my brother Paul, my stepbrother Paul and my stepsister Nicola. It is a blessing that my mother was working.

It must have been around 1982-83, I was living with my mother and my brother and joining us was my stepfamily. Ken, my stepfather, sold his house and moved into my mother's home at Green Lane. He was spending the majority of the money from the sale of his house to renovate our home to accommodate us all. We now had central heating, the first time I had lived in a house with central heating. At this time, I had a dog, a German Shepherd called Kye. My dog was not in the best of health after having an operation. With this and the extra heat of the house, it must have all been a bit too much for the dog and she had urinated on the new carpets. On returning home from work, I was confronted by Ken and we argued about this. Cut to the chase, we had an argument and things got a bit heated; it ended up that I slapped him. That was it–he rang my mother who was out visiting his parents at the time. He told her to come home and as I result, I was told to leave the house.

Having been thrown out, I thought to myself, what do I do now? I walked around aimlessly for a while and I then rang Ann to tell her. Come over to mine she suggested and that I did.

I went over to her house and her parents welcomed me as their son to live there until I got on my feet. I managed to find a flat within about four or five days and I moved there.

That was it. I was out in the big wide world, fending for myself, from now on.

I found a flat and moved in with my dog, who was in a weak state.

Within a week she died. She was not strong enough to survive the operation she had had earlier.

I stayed in the flat until I found that I could not afford it. My dad Geordie said that I could move in with him!!!

Geordie died 13 May 1989, aged 62.

Chapter 4
Christmas 1984

The strike was taking its toll. What I remember and what has not been mentioned, was the donations, given to the miners, from fellow miners in Russia. Yes, the Russian miners sending food parcels and toys over for Christmas. These are people who are probably financially worse off than ourselves, here in England most of the time. I don't think these people were ever recognised or thanked enough for what they had donated. 'Spaseeba' (Thank you in Russian).

Shortly after Christmas, it was my mother's birthday: 15th January. I remember buying a cheap birthday card and taking it to my mother's house. It was late and dark outside. I walked to the door and could hear the TV inside. I quietly lifted the letter box and slowly pushed the card through. It only went in halfway as there was a big heavy curtain hanging over the side of the door to keep the cold air out. I didn't want them to hear, so I left the card half in and half out of the letter box. I thought I had disturbed them, and someone would come to the door. So without looking back, I ran off. The birthday card probably got soaked as I remember it raining heavily on my way home.

I had to borrow money from the brewery to help me open the bar. I got a loan of eight thousand pounds and a grant of two thousand pound which had to be paid back. I bought some tables and chairs and stools from MFI. I bought the cheapest cord carpet I could find, and I had a couple of friends help me build a small bar and a cellar room from bricks and blocks. The toilets were situated outside in the yard, they were cheaply renovated and painted out. The cellar bar was wallpapered and carpeted and had the cheapest of tables, chairs and stools. Thanks to my friend Paul Shucksmith, who was a bricklayer, he knew people in the trade who came at a cheap price. We all mucked in together and got the cellar into a bar ready to open.

I had a good friend Joe Lam, a Chinese mate, and we got together to get the lease from the landlords for a wine bar. Joe was my business partner when I opened. This only lasted a few years, as Joe expected the business to bring in more profit than it did. I bought him out.

When Bubbles first opened and for the next few years, trade was mainly at the weekends. It was not really worth opening the doors during the week, but because I would only be sitting at home with Harry my dog, it was just as easy to put the nights in at work. So, I would take Harry, as he would have been in the house on his own.

Harry was the friendliest dog and customers would come in to see him. I got a local professional photographer to get some photos taken of him. The photos were great and I was really pleased with the way they turned out. Not long after I had his photographs taken, people would bring their children into Bubbles, usually on a Saturday lunch time, just to see the German Shepherd dog. This was odd, I could not understand what the fuss was about. I asked them and they explained there was a shop window along the main street where the photographer had his work advertised. I had a walk along to MacKay's shop and to my surprise–there was a window full of wedding photos. But centred perfectly in the middle was Harry. That's my boy.

Chapter 5
Fancy dress

We had several promotion nights in Bubbles. One year, 'Becks beer' had a promotion where they gave us 48 Becks pint glasses and we were told to serve the Becks beer in these glasses in an attempt to sell more beer. I thought to myself, if we put Becks beer in these glasses, we will not get the glasses back. The brewery had also said that the top ten pubs and clubs would win a prize. The prize was whoever increased their percentage sales of Becks beer would have a trip to the Becks brewery in Bremen, Germany. I was told by my brewery representative, Jack Milburn, that he had been to the Becks brewery and it was out of this world. Not only the brewery visit but the whole trip was top class. I was up for that, so what I decided to do was to reduce the price of Becks beer to the same price as the standard lager; when a customer bought a pint, they would get a free ticket. Once they had collected ten tickets, they would hand them over the bar and receive a free pint glass. This was so successful that my kegs of beer went from one keg per week to 11 or 12 per week over the period of one month. I came out on top–I had the highest percentage increase, but what happened, the sales fell on the normal lager. Obviously, to buy in Becks was more expensive for me, but it wasn't too bad losing a little profit when I won a two-night stay in a five-star hotel in Germany with all expenses paid by Becks Brewery. The hospitality was second to none–beautiful town, amazing brewery and amazing people. On another Becks promotion night, we decided to go for fancy dress, German themed. But a couple of the staff came in original fancy dress–one a clown's outfit, his wife a French maid. I thought when I saw the clown, wouldn't it be funny if there was trouble tonight and the clown had to be serious to help sort it out. Guess what, his wife became harassed by the drunken customers and the clown then had to step up to the mark and confront the drunken men.

Yes. It was funny.

Chapter 6
Staff

It must happen a lot in the bar trade, the temptation of cash and drinks. My first problem arose when I was told by some of my regular customers that members of my staff were giving away pints of beer to regular customers. This was a bit of a long drawn out affair; I tried to see what was happening but could not. So I decided to hire a private detective.

Over the period of a couple of weeks, I had the results. To my horror, not only one of my staff was giving away drinks, but there were three that came back on the report.

There were two guys who would come into the bar at the weekends when we were busy. When they came in, they would stand away from the bar. One of the staff knew their regular tipple. She would pour two pints of beer and place them on the bar and walk away. Within minutes, the two pints would disappear, and the two guys were stood drinking them. This happened up to five or six times during the night. She was named in the report. Another girl was doing the same, but with not as many drinks; she was also named in the report. The third girl apparently gave a relation of hers a couple of free pints. They were all sacked. I tried to take one of them to court, but her father had a good lawyer and we got nowhere.

On another occasion, there was a lad working for me. He came in to help over the Christmas and New Year, having previously worked at holiday camps. He was due to return to the holiday camp in the springtime, ready for the summer trade.

Once again I grew curious of him and I had surveillance cameras on behind the bar. Nothing showed. I later found out he was not ringing the correct amount of money in the till and he was leaving extra cash at the till. When other staff members were using the till, he was back in taking the extra cash out for himself when the till drawer was open.

It was Boxing Day and we were busy again. I had asked a couple of friends who were out socialising to watch him and tell me if they saw anything suspicious; I also asked my doorman to keep a look out. During the night, I would walk over to my detectives and raise my eyebrows as a suggestion of what was happening. But nothing was seen.

As it happens, we had a large safe that was in the area where the staff hung up their coats. The safe was quite discreet and when using the safe, I was hidden from view.

I went to the safe to get some bags of loose change to put in the till, when this lad came in. He didn't know I was there, and I saw him go into his coat and fumble around with a handkerchief, taking it out of his coat and putting it back in. Strange, I thought. Once I had the amount of change I needed, I walked past his coat and felt the outside of his pocket. What I noticed was, I felt a hard lump under his handkerchief. A shiver went down my spine, but I decided to wait until the end of the night before I would approach him. I asked some of my customers (including my detectives for the night) to hang around.

It was payday for the staff, this was the pay for working over the Christmas. I started to hand out all of the pay packets to the staff, but I left this guy's until last. I could see he was eager to get away, but I made him wait. I held his pay packet in my hand and I said to him, "Will you be handing over your pay to me to cover towards the money you've stolen?" He went a deep shade of red and argued back in defence. "What do you mean?" "Well," I said, "you will empty your coat pocket and put the contents on the bar otherwise I will have no choice but to call the police." He started to empty his pockets onto the bar, but what I saw was unbelievable. There were five, ten and twenty pound notes all screwed up into balls. He had just put a pile of money on my bar. There was around one hundred pounds. I asked him how much he had taken over the past few weeks, and he sheepishly replied about three or four hundred pounds. If this is what he admitted, I would have thought it was a lot more. I suggested to him that I would keep his pay packet, and the cash on the bar. I told him I wanted the rest of the money to be returned to me. I reported it all to the police that evening and explained he had agreed to pay me what he had stolen. The following day at around 6pm, I got a telephone call from the police saying they had gone to his house in the early hours of that morning at around 7am and caught him leaving the house with his case packed and a pocket full of cash. The police arrested him, took him to the police cells, holding him there for the rest of the day until around 5pm. He admitted to stealing the money, he handed over the cash that he had on him–which was around three hundred pounds–and agreed for the police to give it back to me. I later got my stock takers report for the Christmas and New Year period and my stock was down by around one thousand pounds.

Was it him? Or was there someone else? Who knows.

Theft in the bar trade is rife. When there are drinks and cash available, the temptation for some people is just too much. Over the years, I have had numerous other occasions where I have caught people stealing.

Chapter 7
Alterations

When I opened Bubbles, it was on a budget and being a cellar to the shops above, it has low ceilings and internally there were walls and archways. Bubbles is a cellar below two shops above, opened up into one larger cellar over the years previous. There must have been originally four rooms. Steel girders supporting the floors above, but what had been there before? Archways for support probably?

I checked them out by knocking away some of the bricks and some of the bits and bobs added over the years. To my amazement, there were four fireplaces with chimneys.

The bar was too small now to serve drinks and the storeroom for the beer and kegs was behind the bar and the tiny kitchen next to them both. Time for a change…

Before the change

Two years have now passed and business is going ok. Weekends are busy and because Bubbles is a small cellar bar, it can get a bit uncomfortable at times. I thought that if I could get the landlord's permission, it would be a good idea to try and make more room for our customers to enjoy, and not just that, there were too many walls and archways and when a band was playing at times it was a bit difficult to see and enjoy them.

Permission was granted and the work was to take place. Once again, I called for my mate Reg to come and have a look.

It was a big job. The building was originally the Station Master's house. The railway line and town centre were just outside. The original building stood alone on what is now Ashington's main street.

There was a lot of structural support on the walls and archways in the cellar, and to remove any of these supports could end in disaster. If any of the building was to move in any way when removing these supporting walls, the whole building could be affected or even collapse.

Part of the work was to build in supporting beams. There were three of these massive RSJ girders which had to be put in place while supporting the two floors above. The only problem was how do we manage to get them up to the height required? Well, simple, actually, all we needed to do was get the help of Bubbles 'Tug of War' team.

We all rallied around without any hesitation, about ten of us. Then we got the girders up to the required height and supported them on scaffold, then slowly manoeuvred them into place. Simple

After the change

when there is a Tug of War team at hand.

The work progressed and a new bar was built, giving the place a new look, but more important, a lot more room.

While I'm on the subject of the building being built as the Station Master's house… It was many things during its time.

Local newspapers were printed here. Portland printers. They had a shop above where they sold their goods including postcards.

A local motor cycle shop had it for a store room, H and H Motor Cycles. Their shop was over the railway bridge, next to the town hall.

The Lamp Glass Cellar Club. Ashington's 'Folk Club'.

Cellar Records, run by yours truly, selling vinyl records, cassette tapes and early days of video tapes were for hire. 'T' shirts, mirrors, posters and other bits and bobs.

Then Bubbles came along and is still there to this day.

I was driving through Newcastle one day and I noticed a place

Above: Bubbles tug of war team
Right: Tug of war trophies

selling flower tubs. This place had old wooden beer casks, cut in half and had put flowers in them.

What a waste. I went in and asked if they had any wooden casks, they hadn't cut. To my luck, there were four large and eight small. They were a perfect height and size to be used as tables and stools. I bought them all and brought them to their new home, where they are still today.

Chapter 8
The pub next door

This was a large property previously used as a Dairy. Run and owned by the Co-op society, it was situated directly behind Bubbles. A very large building which had been run down over the years.

I was in competition with another interested party trying to buy it. The local estate agent who was selling this on behalf of the Co-op, caused problems from the start. It seemed that the other interested party was on friendly terms with the estate agent. This did not arise until a little time down the line. What I found was every time I put an offer in to buy the building, my offer was mentioned to the opposition party who would then up their offer. To my disgust, I was never informed about this. I would be waiting for things to progress, but would hear nothing. I decided to walk into the then fully operating Dairy to speak to the manager. He informed me that there was another higher offer on the table, higher than my offer. I would then ring the estate agent and put in another higher offer, and ask to speak to the person dealing with this, but he was always unavailable.

Co-op dairy and milk men's last shift

I then decided to inform the head office of the Co-op and put my offer in directly to them, instead of the Estate Agent.

To cut a long story short, we had a contract race between myself and the other interested party. I managed to scrape together enough money as a deposit then raced through to my solicitors in Newcastle upon Tyne and told them to get the contract and have it signed.

I did it... This was now the start to a long and enduring few years in converting the Co-op Dairy to The Black Diamond Inn.

Plans were drawn up for me by a gentleman called Jimmy Floyd, who had been introduced to me. His plans were magnificent–they consisted of a large bar, a lounge diner, a restaurant, four letting rooms, large kitchen, a large cellar and an office. With the obvious others such as toilets etc.

This project was massive for me. Someone who has no money, but big ambitions. I managed to arrange loans from Scottish and Newcastle breweries during the different stages of the build.

Phase one was to open the bar and customer toilets, the cellar and build an office to work from. Once again, I called on my good friend Reg Warnes, the joiner, and we managed to get enough bodies together to get the job started.

I need now to mention my stepfather, Ken. Ken and myself had had a rocky start, with my mother and him being married and me being told to leave the house. But over the following ten or so years, things had settled down. We became good friends. Ken was retired from work and had plenty of spare time on his hands. To be quite honest, he was as enthusiastic about the project as myself. Ken and I were in the newly bought premises from the off, labouring away, stripping out all of the internal building and other bits and bobs. I won't bore you with the logistics to the build, which took around seven years to complete, but I must say a big thank you to Ken for being there for me and helping me through it all. He lifted me during the times I was down.

Above: Job started–Reg Warnes, Ronnie Garbet and Paul Shucksmith; Right: Step dad Ken Cook, and uncle Ken Stephen

Ashington Fire brigade, helping with telephone box in the bar

When I started the build, Ken was 67 years old. But he had the drive and the ability of a 25 year old. Another gentleman who became a good friend to me was another man the same age as Ken, called Bob Poxon. Bob was a painter and decorator and his perfection was graining. An art where he could make a plain piece of wood look as though it had been specially varnished, showing all the veins and grains, seen on an expensive piece of wood. Bob would stop working if anyone came into a room he was working in, wait until they left before starting up again; he would not let people see how his work was done. It took years before he showed me.

I managed to open the bar in January 1997.

To follow shortly after was the Lounge/Diner in September of

Above: The Black Diamond lounge; Right: Jenniccas Ristorante-Italian restaurant at The Black Diamond

the same year, 1997.

The strain of trying to convert a large building whilst also trying to start up the new business in the same premises, was at least challenging to say the least, but to be also running a well established bar next door at the same time was definitely demanding.

A year went by and The Black Diamond Inn was taking a good stand in the community. Christmas of 1998 came around, followed by the New Year. This is when we had the high winds.

I remember being in The Black Diamond. The winds were fierce and at one point during service we had to close all the doors, especially the main entrance door.

I heard crashing in the Lounge and as I went in, I saw the whole ceiling moving up and down.

There were chandeliers bouncing up and down with the pressure of the wind getting into the roof area above. I was scared of what might happen.

There were stories of people getting blown onto the road.

Tiles and slates crashing down from roof tops and loose chimney stacks being blown down.

This lasted into the early hours of the next morning.

Next day, as I was to start work, I was approached by my neighbour of The Black Diamond Inn, Kevin Davison, who is a good friend of mine, by the way. Kevin said to me, "Come and have a look and see what the wind has done to my house."

I went with him and he led me to his front living room where he had just had a conservatory built earlier that same year. It was like a building site! The top of the gable end from The Black Diamond Inn had been blown over and had fallen onto his conservatory. Their Christmas tree and most of the children's presents were totally destroyed.

"Shit," I said, also worrying about what might have happened to my pub. I said that I would get in touch with my insurance company. "No problem," Kevin said, "There's nothing we can do, at least the kids weren't playing in there at the time as they had been later in the night before."

I then went into The Black Diamond not knowing what to expect. The Lounge had survived, with only a couple of marks where some of the bricks had fallen onto the ceiling above.

I then went upstairs to find that I could see daylight through the roof.

There had been a large 'Dutch Gable' design on the end of the building, which had stood through two world wars, but was unfortunately defeated by the winds the night before.

Luckily, the upstairs was vacant. This was to be the next phase of the development, letting rooms. Can you imagine what could have happened if these rooms had been completed and were being used by guests?

Once the situation was sorted and time rolled on, the work began to build the guest rooms. Top of the list was to remove the 'Dutch gable' and make the building more safe.

The guest rooms, four in total, were completed and open in 1999.

Then the restaurant was open in 2002.

This whole project took around seven years to complete.

Ken died 2014, aged 85

Bob died 2016, aged 87

Chapter 9
The uninvited guest

One incident I recall which took place in The Black Diamond Inn.

There were letting rooms and we often had business people passing through the area.

It is important not to take your finger off the button, or so they say. The two pubs were becoming busier than ever, and I had to rely on staff to take over if myself or the manager, Paul Gray, were not available. Well just that happened, both Paul and myself were unaware of this chap who had managed to persuade one of the supervisors in The Black Diamond Inn, to run up a bill. He said he was in the area to recruit some workers to be involved in a new project in the next town of Newbiggin-by-the-Sea. He said that an old farm was to be renovated and he was to find suitable local workers. He wanted to interview them in the bar and he booked himself into a room for two or three nights. He arrived on a Friday, had meals and drinks put onto his account, and on the Saturday, he was seen in the bar interviewing some local lads. This took a few hours. He was a friendly chap, or so I'm told, he got on well with the staff. On the Saturday we had a wedding reception booked in the restaurant. The wedding party had booked the whole restaurant for the day and evening. They were lovely people and they all had a great time. Somehow, mingling with the crowd and being involved with the wedding party was this guy. He was seen talking to people and even ended up on some of the photographs! He was later seen in Bubbles, and he partied until the early hours. When I came to work on the Sunday morning, I heard the staff talking about this chap. I then realised he was running up a bill. "Who gave permission for this?" I said. "We don't even have his credit card details." I was furious. I then went up to his room as he had not turned up for breakfast. I knocked on the door and told him to open up. No answer. Again, I said "open up or I will open up with our spare key". Still no answer. I put the key in the lock and opened the door. What a mess. The room was stinking. The bed was untidy and the en-suite light and extractor fan were still on. Guess what!! He had done a runner through the night. He hadn't paid his bill and to top it off, he had pissed the bed. He left, leaving all the food and drinks he had under his false name. Hmmm. I wonder if he had parked in another car park. Well, I had to put it down to experience. We tightened up all future bookings after this.

Chapter 10
Halloween

We would celebrate Halloween in Bubbles with something or another arranged. We would often hire a live band called Spook and the Ghouls. These guys would dress up and play a bit of rock music. They were entertaining and always went down well with the crowd. Some occasions, we would have a fancy dress night. I remember one evening, me and my brother Paul decided to dress up for the evening. It was quite funny as I went out and bought a mask and put on a chef's jacket covered in fake blood and trousers to match. My brother turned up at my house, with a wet-look plastic coat on, his head completely wrapped up in a bandage. He had two holes for eyes, covered with a pair of sunglasses which kept falling off because he had no ears to keep them on. He also had a tiny hole where his mouth was to breathe a little.

Off we went to Bubbles Halloween party. It didn't take people long before they could tell it was me... but nobody knew who the invisible man was (maybe they couldn't see him?). Everyone who was in fancy dress that evening went up on stage and the customers had to cheer for the best dressed. When the invisible man was called up, the whole pub cheered. Paul had won! What a laugh. Soon as the competition was over, my brother Paul had to take off all the bandages and reveal his identity.

Chapter 11
HMRC

When I opened Bubbles, I went to the college where they had a business course–BII, British Institute of Innkeeping. This was a great course to be on as it explained how to run a pub, get to know how all beer is brewed and how spirits are distilled. It also explained about keeping correct books (accounts). It gave a good outline to the do's and don'ts in the bar trade.

But what it didn't tell me was what was about to happen next.

I had been open, coming up to two years and my accounts were to be handed into the tax office. I had a local accountant who had been taking care of my accounts and wages for me to allow me to concentrate on building up the bar trade. My accounts went into the tax office and there were a couple of queries. I spoke to my accountant and he said that the tax man wants you to go in to see him. I asked why as I had not been doing my accounts. I asked my accountant to go in on my behalf. At that time, my accountant had a new business partner, a young chap who was a 'computer expert'. He was sent to see the tax man, and he came back and told me that the tax man was not happy with my accounts. He said that he suspected I should be paying more tax. Apparently, the books were incorrect, and it looked like I had not declared all of my takings. The accountant had agreed I should pay a small fine and a bit of extra tax.

Well, as you can imagine, I was furious. I said to him, you have all of my till readings and receipts. You have done my accounts and said they were ok before we agreed to send them in. I told him that he had admitted to something which had never happened. I refused to accept it, and I appealed. This was the start of a six-year-long appeal.

I went through three accountants and found how bad things could get. I had one of the accountants lose receipts, saying they had never received them. Strange?

At that time, I was reading in the newspapers how tax inspectors worked on commission for any additional tax collected. What I mean by that, I had newspaper cuttings saying that the Inland Revenue had introduced a system where if a tax inspector could get more tax from someone after they had paid their tax, the tax inspector would be on a percentage of the extra money collected as a bonus. Illegal...

It all came to an end when I had an accountant who knew a lady who was a retired tax inspector. She worked as a tax consultant. She would see fair play between a client and the Inland Revenue. My accountant was based in Derby and this lady in Nottingham. We arranged a meeting with her at her office. She gave me the full grilling of a tax inspector. At the end of my visit, I got up out of my chair and said, "If this is what being self-employed is about,

I will have to go bankrupt." I then turned and walked out of her office and back to the car. She let me go, and followed me. She then came over to the car and said come back inside and let us have a more friendlier chat. I had to let you go to see if I believed you. I do believe you and I would like to take your appeal and see if I can help you, or words to that effect. Well, by this time I had given up and said to her "forget it". She gently smiled at me and said, "You have gone through a lot and I think you have a very good case." What I forgot to mention was a few months earlier I had been skiing in Scotland for a weekend. I had a bad accident which put me in hospital. I had been knocked off the ski slope and down into some rocks on the cliff side. I had five fractures in my head and I dislodged my inner ear, breaking a bone in my right ear. I am now totally deaf in the right ear and my balance is horrendous.

During the next year, I had a meeting with both Mrs J (my consultant) and Mr X, the tax inspector, in his office. This was my second meeting with him, my first was with another accountant who was absolutely hopeless. I sacked him in the tax office and walked out. Anyway, getting back to my meeting with him and Mrs J, we went in and he was not pleased with me to say the least. The meeting lasted around 30-40 mins, and during this time Mrs J said very little and the tax man was becoming more and more aggressive. She tipped me a wink, reassuring me. We left and she said, leave it with me.

Shortly after, I received a letter from Inland Revenue saying it would be taking me to the High Court in London and on the letter was the date to attend. I contacted Mrs J and she calmly said, "That is fine, if they take you to court, they must attend themselves. But we can send in a letter. Leave it to me."

The court date came and went. Shortly after, I received a letter from Inland Revenue saying all charges against me had been dropped.

I was ecstatic. I rang Mrs J and thanked her for everything she had done. I said even though I was pleased we had been proven to be right and won the case, it should never have happened in the first place. Was there anything I could do, for example write to the tax man's boss at Inland Revenue and express my disappointment?.

"Yes," she said, "write a letter and address it to the district inspector but do not send it, let me read it first." This I did, I sent the letter saying I had experienced six years plus, of hell and thanks to the high court it has now been resolved. I hope to have a better relationship with the Inland Revenue in the future.

I sent this off to Mrs J. She replied having read it and told me to send it.

A few days later, a letter arrived from the district inspector. Four pages saying that Mr X was correct in what he did and that he could not see how he should apologise.

I never asked for an apology. I rang Mrs J and told her. "Send me the letter," she said, and I did so immediately. That was the last I heard.

When my next tax return form arrived, I noticed there was a new district inspector. Strange? I had also heard through the grapevine that Mr X had been moved on… "promoted" I was told.

What a weight off my shoulders. I could concentrate with

building the business up, now the world was my oyster. I could move forward.

I always wanted to own my own pub. Bubbles was a lease with landlords at the helm. Even though I was free trade, Bubbles was still not my building. I remember asking the landlords if I could build a small extension to the back of the building and add some inside toilets. They asked for my plans to look over to see how much extra rent they would have to charge. What!… I was going to pay for the building work and undoubtedly going to improve the value of their property and for the pleasure of doing so, they would increase my rent? Forget it.

Chapter 12
Back to Bubbles

usic was my first love and bringing acts to the folk of Ashington was my aim. I remember asking an old school mate of mine when I first opened the bar, "What would you think about playing at Bubbles with your band Rhythm Method?" Malcom Fox was the lead singer in the band. "Get a diary and get at least six to seven bands signed up to cover your first few weeks and others will want to play. They will start ringing you," said Malcom.

I had been open about ten months before I had my first live band playing on Thursday nights. The interest was great, both the bands liked playing and the customers flocked to listen. I think because Bubbles is a cellar bar, it has a good sound and ambiance. Remember the Beatles started off playing in the Cavern in Liverpool.

Also, the folk club had its share of big names. I remember seeing that the 'Humble Bums' played. That was the 'Big Yin' Billy Connolly and Gerry Rafferty. Also the original 'Fleetwood Mac' with Peter Green. That was before the Americans joined, Stevie

Nicks and Lindsey Buckingham. A lot of people from the sixties, not forgetting Don Partridge and the Spinners, Alexis Korner and Tiny Tim, just to mention a few.

I would get the odd 'named' band which would cost a lot of money, a lot more than any local bands. My cousin, Michael Stephen, is a promoter/agent. He moved away from the North East when he was a kid as his parents had to move for work purposes. Michael is like a brother to me, we had been close since kids, playing together and sleeping at each other's houses. Anyway, back to the bands. Michael would have a lot of bands who had played in the earlier years, on his books.

I managed to book the mighty Groundhogs to play. They were my heroes when I was a young lad and getting into real music.

Around 1973 I remember going to watch The Groundhogs at Alexandra Palace in London when I was 15 years old. Myself, with Malcom Fox and Peter Swanson. We told our parents we were staying at each other's aunt's house in London, but we slept on a park bench. If we could even call it sleep. Getting back to The Groundhogs. I managed to get them booked to play at Bubbles, and I got to meet my hero, Tony McPhee. The band were fantastic and Bubbles was packed. What a great night. We all sat behind and had a couple of drinks before going back to my house to have a Chinese take-away supper which I collected from my

Groundhogs ticket

good friend Alex Shek.

Fancy that–having a Chinese meal with The Groundhogs in my house! They ended up playing three times in all in Bubbles.

The last time they came, I had an unplugged night in Bubbles. This was when I had a full stage set up with drums, lead guitar and amp, bass guitar and amp, acoustic guitar and microphones, all fed through a PA system. Anyone could get up on the night. We had some great nights.

The Groundhogs rang one Sunday afternoon and asked if they could play that evening. Even though they were my heroes, remember, I said that they could not as I would not be able to get it advertised and get their fee in time. Also, to top it off, it was our unplugged night. They said they only wanted somewhere to sleep as they had played The Aberdeen Blues Festival on the Saturday, then were off to Liverpool, playing on the Monday. Ashington seemingly fit in the middle. I said if they wanted, they could crash at my house. They agreed.

Later that day, I opened Bubbles at 7pm and shortly after that, in walked the Groundhogs. They had travelled from Scotland for around seven hours. I told the staff in Bubbles that I would be back later. They came to my house, freshened up, and I took them for a drink in a local bar before going to Bubbles. When we walked into Bubbles, word had already got around Ashington and the pub was jam packed. A couple of guys were up playing when we walked in. After about an hour or so, The Groundhogs said to me "Can we play?" What???

They got up on stage and played with the equipment that was

already there. They were fantastic. They played non-stop for two hours. I did not know that I could get such a good sound from the equipment I already had on the stage.

The so called 'Unplugged Nights' were on a Sunday night. After practising with the band that I was playing with, I would leave the drum kit set up and put in a Bass amp and guitar, a Lead amp and guitar, an acoustic guitar and microphones all put through a PA system.

Anyone could get up and play. Many a time a couple of the guys would rally around with other customers and scratch a band together. They would jam all unrehearsed and there was many a good tune played. Some of the folk were quite good, some played in other bands and some were just a 'would be' musician.

There was one guy who would come in now and again, he was called Davey Mears 'Day Day' was his nickname. He was an up and coming drummer. As many of us will know, the drums are the most unsociable instrument, especially when they are not played with a particular rhythm. Well, Davey was one of those. He would come in early, most of the time it was just after opening, and would ask, "Is it ok if I get up on the drums?" Well that was the whole purpose of the night. It was a bit painful, I must admit , but people would warm to his enthusiasm.

Mick Abrahams, Cheryl Beer, Mick Pinney, Greg Wright were a few names. Also Doctor and the Medics, Eddie and the Hot Rods all played in Bubbles. My cousin Michael and Cheryl were on the road a few times touring the UK.

This brings me to Bob Geldof. Bob never played Bubbles,

but my cousin Michael was his promoter for years. When Bob's manager died, Michael was then managing Bob and the boys.

I met up with them a couple of times when they came to Newcastle and Middlesbrough. I saw first-hand how hard it is to be on the road.

I managed to give it a go playing in a couple of bands. It started off one night before Christmas when I was in Bubbles with a couple of lads at the end of my shift. My brother Paul was learning the guitar at home at the time and the conversation got on about music and playing the guitar. One of the lads in our company, Alan Armstrong, said, "I can play the lead guitar. Why don't we start a band?" We all laughed. "Paul, you can learn the bass guitar and Dave, you can play the drums. Kevin, you sing." We decided amongst each other, in our semi-drunken state. It's funny how drinks can take over and by the end of the night I had managed to borrow a set of drums for practice. "We will learn one song and play it here in Bubbles on New Year's Eve," said the lads. That was it, agreed. We learned *Just What I Needed*, by The Cars. We were up on New Year's Eve and played our one song. That was it. Over.

It ignited a passion to learn more stuff, however. We went on to play a bank holiday at Bubbles, the first band to play out of eight bands on the day. We were outside in the back yard. It went well. I think we did one more bank holiday before we folded.

I went on to play with another band, Midnight Express, with my good friend Reg Warnes. Reg was my school pal and joiner. One of the best. We got together with two other guys who were musicians, Alan Potts and Malcom Douglass. We played a bank holiday Monday and shortly after, split up with Malcom Douglass and in stepped big Richie. Once again, played a bank holiday Monday, a few Sunday nights then went on tour.

My cousin Michael lives in South Wales. He arranged for us to play six gigs over seven days. What an experience.

A few years went by and I was talking to a good friend who I met through him playing in bands over the years, Bob Davison. He was probably the best singer I've heard and he could play the guitar as well. Bob wanted somewhere to practice and I suggested he could use Bubbles in the afternoon on Sundays as the bar was closed. By this time, I had just opened my second bar, The Black Diamond Inn. Bob agreed and before long, he asked me if I wanted to play drums for a few of his songs just to give it a bit of a beat. Well yes… I started practising with Bob and before we knew it, we were playing as a band. Bob Davison, Graham Kelly, Alek Ola and myself. We got together and it was going great.

Bob said he knew a lad who could play the harmonica/Blues harp and wanted to get him involved. This guy was Mike Harris.

Bob got Mike to call along and the band was complete. 'Smokestack Lightnin' we were called. It's the name of an old

Howlin' Wolf song. Mike came up with the name. We were a band for four years or so, playing in

Life on the road, sleeping under a pool table

*Above: Newbiggin by the
sea; Right: Smokestack
lightenin' in Bubbles*

decent venues such as
Aberdeen Blues Festival where two bands did not turn up at our
booking so we ended up playing for around five hours then drove
straight back home. What...

We supported John Rossall's Glitter Band (this guy was in Garry
Glitter's band). We played in Newbiggin's Sport Centre, then the
next day, we supported Geno Washington and the Ram Jam Band
on an open air stage at Newbiggin Bay in front of around 4000
people. What an experience.

Chapter 13
HMRC again

The trouble is, when trying to write a book, things happen. When you write about them, other things are also happening at the same time.

During the years of playing in bands, the business was also facing a couple of problems. Yes, Inland Revenue again.

One afternoon, I was not at work and I was out with my two dogs for a walk. Bearing in mind, this was before mobile phones were popular. I took the dogs past Bubbles so I could just pop in and check on everything. I no sooner turned the corner, on the home straight, heading towards Bubbles, when I saw Ann running towards me, shouting my name." David," she cried, "you need to come quickly; we have a tax collector and a bailiff in the bar. They said they are going to take away goods and stock." I ran into the bar and there they were. A man and woman stood at the bar. "Can I help?" I asked. "Well if you pay this bill it might help," said the woman, then handing me a slip. The bill was a demand for a non-payment of PAYE. "I'm sure I have paid," I said. "Not according to this," she uttered sarcastically. I went into the safe to get my chequebook out, fumbling through shaking. The demand was for four thousand, six hundred and eighty something pounds. A large amount of money. I found I had regular monthly payments to the Inland Revenue for my PAYE in my chequebook slips. "Is this amount what I've already paid been deducted?" I asked. She didn't know. Well, I thought, what are you doing here if you don't know what has and what hasn't been paid? "Who is this?" I asked, as I pointed to the man beside her. "This is the bailiff," she explained. "BAILIFF??? Where is my reminder and red letter before any action is taken?" I said. She did not reply. I then rang my accountant; he was also confused and said to leave it with him. I repeated this to both of them as they stood in front of me. She gave me her card and said I had to get in touch with her first thing the next day. They both turned and left the bar.

The next day, my accountant rang me back. He said the Inland Revenue had got things wrong, having mixed up the wrong account number associated with Bubbles. I hastily rang the number on the card given to me the previous day and asked to speak to the tax collector. "Sorry, she's not in at the moment," the man replied. "Not in? She said I had to ring first thing today?" I then went on to explain what had happened. It took a while, but he eventually said, "It was a computer error!!!"

Chapter 14
VAT

And yet another blunder from Inland Revenue

A red letter this time! I had received a VAT demand from Inland Revenue to be paid immediately otherwise action would be taken to recover the full amount.

I had tried to ring to sort this one out myself but found I could not get any sense. I went to see my MP, who at the time was Mr Jack Thompson (now deceased). I made an appointment with Mr Thompson and showed him the letter. I also explained my previous encounters with TAX and PAYE. "Leave this with me," he said and I did just that.

A week or so later, he asked to see me. I went to his surgery and he gave me a full written apology from the VAT office. Mr Thompson had gone into their office and told them my predicament. "A computer error," he told me. I think that the Inland Revenue must have bought a job lot of computers all from the same place as they all seemed to have the same fault. It's funny that it's not the person putting the information into the computer that's at fault.

I had one more visit to the tax office during my time in Bubbles and The Black Diamond and I took my accountant in with me to avoid a return visit.

Things went ok I'm pleased to say.

Chapter 15
Characters

I am sure that all the pubs and bars in and around the country, or even the world, have their fair share of characters. I remember when I went to the magistrates to apply for my licence in 1985, there was a chap in the gallery watching. He came into Bubbles on the opening night, Saturday 13th April 1985. He was a very well spoken gentleman who wore a big thick beard with a cigarette in one hand and a drink in the other. He introduced himself by saying "Congratulations on getting your licence". "Thank you," I said; he then replied, "I was in the gallery. I am pleased you managed to get your licence and open Bubbles. We need more pubs in Ashington."

There have been only three pubs in the town amongst 27 licenced premises. These included a football club, the rugby club, the cricket club. The rest were CIU working men's clubs.

Apparently, there was a by-law on the town, years before, by the chap who was titled the Duke of Portland. He was putting covenants on all properties to stop them from obtaining a public house licence. This was in the early days of the town when it was occupied by miners and their families. Before the mines were nationalised, the miners had to support their families whether they were at work or not. There was no NHS in those days.

Groups of miners got together and had their own smaller groups who then applied to open private clubs. A miner would join one of these clubs and pay a contribution. They would socialise in their club and the profits were there to help the families of the man/ miner of the house if anything should happen. Health and safety at work was not what it is today.

This in one sense was the opposite of what the Duke of Portland had in mind, when he tried to not encourage the man of the house to be out drinking and in turn have time off work. There were three pubs at the time. There were the Grand Hotel, the Portland Arms Hotel and the North Seaton Hotel–the latter was nicknamed 'The White Elephant'. I was told it got this nickname as it never seemed to make any profit, but it kept on going.

When Bubbles opened in April 1985, another two bars followed shortly after. In the month of June, that same year, Benny's Bar opened and was followed in July by The Great Oak. Within three months, the total number of public houses had doubled from three to six.

Times were moving forward.

Chapter 16
Ron

Back to the chap with the beard who congratulated me on my opening night. His name was Ron Wood. Not to be mistaken with the guy from the Rolling Stones.

Ron ended up being a long and regular customer. He and his wife Joan must have been around about 50 plus when they came in the early days. I can honestly say they were in most days as soon as we opened the doors. He went around most of the CIU clubs as a stock-taker and bookkeeper. He would do his work in each of the clubs and then call in at Bubbles before going home to sort out their businesses.

For years he asked to be my bookkeeper and stock-taker but we kept our relationship strictly pleasurable.

Ron would bring in a lot of customers over the years. There would be a bunch of them all standing around the bar, all giving me advice on how I should run my bar. In fact, I'm sure some of them must have been unemployed solicitors. Not…

God help me if I'd taken some of the advice.

Ron Wood, I remember one occasion, Ron had been in one

of the CIU clubs in Ashington stock-taking. I believe that Ron, a cleaner and the Steward to the club, were all in the club at the same time when a gang broke into the club. Ron and the cleaner were forced to lie down on the floor of the bar with a gun to their head, while the Steward was taken by the gang members to the safe. I'm not sure of the exact details but apparently the police had the whole area surrounded and managed to catch the culprits. Ron was late in Bubbles that day, obviously, and was quite shaken about the whole ordeal before he explained what had happened.

He was a regular drinker and smoker. Smoking was allowed in bars up until 2007. That's when the smoking ban came in. It was the norm to see people in bars with a drink and cigarette, especially Ron.

I think what a lot of the smokers did not recognise, was when they stood or sat at the bar, they would blow smoke over the bar and towards the working bar staff.

It was in the early part of the year of 2007 around March when I had a regular visit from the environmental health officer. The main talking point was how to introduce the smoking ban which would be in force by 1st July that same year. The government were about to enforce a ban on smoking inside of all public places.

The environmental health officer suggested that I put up some signs on the bar counter telling customers not to smoke at the bar. This would be the start of the enforcement which was soon to follow. I agreed to do this, I set out and made some signs to be placed at the bar saying 'due to government legislation to be enforced this year, we request customers not to smoke at the bar'.

Well, one Sunday lunchtime, I was working in The Black Diamond and in walked Ron and his wife Joan. Ron saw the signs; he was not happy. He let his feelings be known to the staff and the customers. "You are taking away my rights," he said to the staff. "It is NOT government legislation, poppy-cock," he growled. He ordered drinks for himself and Joan and took out a cigarette. He walked away from the bar and lit it up. He took a couple of puffs from the cigarette, placed it in the ash tray on a table nearby and walked back to the bar, taking a drink of his freshly pulled pint. He walked back to the table taking a few more puffs of his cigarette.

This continued for a while and all of this time his building rage became apparent. A volcano ready to erupt. I walked into the bar, blissfully unaware of this. His wife Joan was sitting at the bar on a bar stool and Ron was angrily smoking his cigarette away from the bar. I said "Hello" to Joan and a couple of other customers as I walked behind the bar. I heard a growling voice shout "Legal legislation!!! poppy-cock". I turned around and there was Ron standing next to his wife. Ron was raging with anger and he gave me a verbal thrashing.

I tried to explain numerous times what had happened, but he was having none of it. It was all about enjoying his time at the bar, having a drink and a cigarette.

By this time, other customers would chip in and tell Ron that in other areas, like indoor shopping centres etc., there was already a ban. Comments that fuelled the fire. I sharply told Ron, albeit it bluntly, that he was a self-centred arsehole. The bar went quiet. I could not believe what happened next. His wife Joan literally fell off her bar stool onto the floor. One lad's drink ended up on the floor and within minutes everyone was giggling.

Ron and myself were left to fight another day. We often disagreed on a lot of things. He was always trying to put his accountant head on. I never took it seriously. We were good mates for all those years that I knew him.

Ron took ill a couple of times. On one occasion, he was taken to hospital with having a heart attack. Joan was left at home on her own. Ron would be the one with the purse-strings, in control of everything they did. What they had to eat, when they would go on holiday etc. This was a shock to Joan's system; she could not cope.

We in Bubbles were obviously concerned about them both.

We had not seen Joan for days. One of my senior staff in Bubbles, Avril, being extremely concerned, went to their house to find it all locked up. She knew something was wrong. Avril tried to get in, but to no avail. She contacted the police and the doctors, who broke into the house to find Joan lying in bed in a poor state. What happened next, was that Avril took Joan to her own house and began to nurse her back to good health. If I am right, this was over a period of a few weeks. Avril would come to work, then go home to take care of Joan.

When Ron was fit enough to be released from hospital, what he did next was ridiculous. He jumped in a taxi from the hospital with no money, got dropped off at Bubbles and asked his mate to lend him some money. He paid for the taxi then he came straight back to the bar to ask for a pint of beer. Avril was behind the bar and said to Ron, "Do you not want to see your wife first?" He demanded a pint. "She is at my house," said Avril. He had a couple of grunts and groans then went over to finish his drink with his mates.

Ron's health deteriorated after a few years. He ended up housebound and lo and behold, so did Joan.

I went to visit him and saw they had carers going in daily. This was their life.

Ron died in 2009. At the crematorium there were few people there, no priest present as Ron was not a believer. It was Ron's carer who was to say a few words to send him off, but he nervously came over to me asking me to say a few words as well.

It put me on the spot, but I then remembered a story I was told about Ron.

The carer struggled with his emotional farewell speech, then I got up and took my place on the rostrum and told a story of Ron being in a rugby team in his early years.

One day the team were to play and they were short of one player, Ron... Ron hadn't turned up for the game. The whole team were in their strip on the pitch with one player missing when a motorcycle came tearing across the field. Yes, it was Ron. He had been drinking the night before and slept in for the game.

Hurriedly, he got ready for the game, still drunk.

I don't know what was the outcome of the game.

Chapter 17
Dave

Then there were my mates who would come in. One in particular, Dave Nixon. I started school with Dave and we were always in each other's class throughout school until we left. We would call and seek each other out on the way to school through the years. Whoever lived the furthest away would call on the other. Dave and his younger brother Geoff.

Dave was the type who was allergic to work. I don't think he had ever worked a day in his life and yet he was one of the brightest lads in the class.

He was for years known around the town always riding his push bike. He would go on long runs to Rothbury and surrounding places. He would say "I'm going on my route"–that was a ride around Lynemouth and Cresswell. A total of 12 miles or so. Summer, winter, rain or snow he was always on that bike. He even entered cycle races, he would turn up at the race wearing his Barbour jacket with his cigs in his pocket while others had their racing shorts, shoes and matching tops, helmets and energy drinks. Not Dave. He was definitely a one-off. His party trick was setting his hair on fire. Yes I know… But he boasted that he never went to the barbers. He would trim his hair by setting it on fire.

I remember, it was around about 1990 and video cameras were quite new. I bought one and lo and behold, I had him come knocking on my door telling me to get the camera out as he was "ganna set his self ahad"–translated, meant set himself on fire.

We went into my garden and there he would perform the same act, over and over. This led him to go further afield up to Rothbury, diving into the river with his crash helmet on from his moped that he had at the time. A scenic place near Rothbury called Thrum Mill.

Getting back to my house. I picked up the video camera and we went into my front garden. Ann, my brother Paul and a few others were there at the time. We went out into the garden, where he stood in front of the camera, and he introduced himself as if he was on TV. "Hello my name is Vidal Sassoon, I've come here to set me sel ahad." We were all chuckling away, watching him. "I'm a professional barber," he said, while trying to light a cigarette he had just rolled. Once he lit the cigarette, he then put the lighter to his hair. It was quite a windy day and as soon as his hair caught fire, it

was blown out. After several attempts, he had a couple of 'good ones' when the flames were quite well lit.

Dave preforming his act at a tug of war competition

I put this video on the TV screens in Bubbles while the background music was being played. People came from miles around to see this crazy bloke. Everyone wanted a copy of the video and before long, it went viral. People were watching it in Australia, even sent to some TV station. The TV programme said they could not play it for obvious reasons, but what a good laugh they had watching it themselves.

I would record him doing his bits and bobs and play them on the TV screens I had around Bubbles. These would bring people in from near and afar.

Dave and his brother Geoff had a little boat with an outboard motor. Kept at Newton-by-the-sea. They were both keen fishermen.

One morning they went out fishing. They took the boat out with fishing rods and a can of petrol. Daft as it was, they had no life jackets, no flare gun and off they went across the horizon. The fish were there and they had a boat-full. "Time to go back!" was suggested. "What are you talking about?" said Dave. "The fish are here so let's get them." Typical of him, if you gave him something for nothing, he would want two.

There was a boat full of fish, time was getting on and the sea started to swell, but that did not stop him from fishing.

After a while, they decided to head back to shore. Once they could find it that is. They had drifted quite a way south from where they had set out. Heading back after a little while, "that's Dunstanburgh Castle" said Dave, "we want to be North of that". By this time, the waves were quite high and the sea was choppy. In fact, the waves had started to come over into the boat. With the small out-board engine working flat out, they were getting nowhere. They started to panic.

It ended up that they threw a lot of the fish back out into the sea so that they could make the boat light enough to be pushed back by the motor. A struggle to say the least, but at least they made it back. Even if it was probably with less than half the fish.

On another occasion I saw Geoff selling fish to the market traders on the shore. Geoff putting boxes of fish onto the scales and talking to the buyer while Dave was on the opposite side of the scales with his foot on, pushing more weight to make it heavier.

Dave McKay, a good friend of mine and still is. A real close pal of mine over the years, we had a spell of coming into Bubbles on a Sunday over the years when the bar was closed to do a bit of boxing training. Other lads who were there were my brother Paul, stepbrother Paul (also known as Chooks), Kevin Davison, Geoff Nixon and Alan Holloway. These lads mostly, but on some occasions others would pop by. I did a little boxing in my early days, starting at around 12 years old and it did come in handy as you will find out later.

A lad in my class at school called Colin McQuade was a boxer and his dad used to train us at the old Miners Welfare; his dad was called Jock McQuade.

Chapter 18
Biff

Another character who appeared on the scene was Chris Buglass (Biff). It's funny how people just seem to appear amongst the company of people and you feel as though they have been there for years. Biff was one of those. He could play the guitar and piano, and did so very well.

Over the years this led him to writing his own stuff. I'm sure one of his songs, humorous I must add, is still on YouTube, titled *Too many pasties, by Biff*.

He wore Jam Jar glasses and I'm sure he had Tourette's, even when singing.

He wrote a few humorous songs, one called *Skidded*, a copy of the music from Don McLean's *Vincent*. He then wrote another one, called *Santa's Bollocks*, a rendition he came up with especially for Christmas.

I remember taking Biff to a show at Newcastle Playhouse. This was promoted by my cousin Michael.

Michael asked if I knew anyone who could come to the show and make sure that all the guitars were in tune during the show. I asked Biff. "Yes," he replied anxiously. "There will be £50 in it for you, Michael had said." The act on the night was 'Three Men and Black'. This was JJ Burnell from the Stranglers, Bruce Foxton from 'The Jam', Jake Burns from 'Stiff Little Fingers' and Pauline Black from 'Selector'. Very experienced people as you can see. "What they need is to make sure all of the guitars are in tune during the show as they don't have time to waste."

Biff and myself went to meet Michael. When we got there, Biff was asked to go through behind the stage to meet the artists.

Just before the show started, Michael came to me and said, "Who the hell is this Biff?" "What's wrong?" I replied. "He's only got an old tuning fork to tune the guitars," he replied, a bit annoyed!!. Well, that was Biff.

He was a chef at Ashington hospital for years. He applied at The Black Diamond for the Chef's position and I gave him the job in my kitchen. A damn good chef I must say, but his only problem was drink.

Over his time of being a chef, we had numerous disagreements and unfortunately, he finally had to go.

The problem was, I had heard just before he had left working at the hospital, Biff had gone into the manager's office and when the manager was on a fortnight's holiday, he put some fish skins behind the radiator and unleashed a couple of boxes of live crickets. I was slightly worried.

My saviour was Bubbles as he did not want to get barred from there–Bubbles was his life.

Chapter 19
Tony

The first time I met Tony, he was working for an amusement company, called Club Amusements. They supplied gaming machines, juke boxes and pool tables to the licensed trade. I must have had a couple of gaming machines in Bubbles for a year or so, when a new face from the company turned up to repair a machine. This was a lad in his early twenties, who came in and started to repair the machine. Talk… My god. I have never heard anybody talk as much. Within minutes, he had an audience. He had members of staff and public in hysterics; something I found later just emphasises his ability to talk. Before he left, he had arranged to come back to fit a burglar alarm into Bubbles; this was his second job.

I was to become very good friends with Tony over the next few years.

On one occasion I remember him delivering a gaming machine, on a Sunday when Bubbles was closed during the day.

This particular Sunday, I was catching up on jobs and painting the outside yard, putting up some hanging baskets. This day, Tony had exchanged one of the gaming machines and before he left he came over. We were chatting. I was telling him how the day before I had fallen out with my girlfriend Ann. We were in the middle of a conversation when a car pulled up at the back gates and all my clothes came flying into the yard, landing on the picnic benches and the yard floor. Ann had arrived; but because we had fallen out, she decided to return my clothes.

This was the first time in my life I had seen Tony not utter a single word. Ann got out of her car, stormed into Bubbles and returned a couple of minutes later with a bag full of money she had taken out of the safe, the whole week's takings. She got into her car and sped off. I turned around and looked at Tony. To my amazement he had painted almost half the yard. "Apart from that, is everything else alright?" he said sarcastically.

On another occasion, Tony popped into Bubbles for a drink. It was a Monday night. There were a handful of customers at the bar and once again, Tony was up to his old tricks. Every time the phone rang, the bar staff would answer by saying "Hello, Bubbles Wine Bar". On that particular evening, the supervisor working was a lad called Dave Cobbledick.

Dave was the type of guy who liked to do things as pedantically as possible. The phone rang on a couple of times and on answering Dave would say "Good evening, Bubbles Wine Bar". This seemed to tickle Tony's sense of humour. So unbeknown to anyone, Tony had the telephone number for Bubbles on speed dial on his mobile.

Tony selected Bubbles, and put his mobile back in his pocket. The phone would ring. "Hello, Bubbles Wine Bar," said Dave

Cobbledick. He hesitated, but no answer. Then put the phone down. No sooner would it ring again. Dave would walk over repeating this again. No reply. Put the phone down and walked away. This must have happened about six or seven times. When I looked over I saw Tony giggling a bright shade of red, tears streaming down his cheeks. Again, the process repeated, continuing for about a dozen times in fifteen minutes. Everyone in the bar could see what was happening, except for Dave, who at this point was getting annoyed to say the least. What made the whole thing so funny was how he remained calm and collected, answering the phone in a professional manner each time. We could not contain ourselves; we were all in hysterics.

I don't know what was more funny, the fact that Dave Cobbledick was unaware, or just the state of Tony standing at the bar, crying with laughter.

I am still best friends with Tony to this day, having survived a few holidays with him.

Chapter 20
Breweries

I am grateful to Scottish and Newcastle Breweries for their involvement over the years. It was thanks to them at the start for both Bubbles and again The Black Diamond, they were happy to help with loans etc.

What I did find out during the years was that I could borrow money and pay it back through barrelage discount. This was ideal for me at the time when I needed to build up the trade and not have to worry about loan repayments.

How barrelage discounts work. The brewery would lend the money and deduct an amount back for themselves with every barrel of beer, lager or cider sold. I would be sold a product for the full amount as on a price list. I would receive a discount from this price for myself and the breweries would retain another amount for the repayment. As Bubbles was a 'free trade bar' this meant that I could use whatever brewer I wanted.

Breweries would 'tie' you down where they could. This was so that I could not put other breweries' products in my bar.

Other breweries would try and offer better discounts from time to time, to try and get their products in the bar.

I did change breweries over the years. I began with Scottish and Newcastle, then Cameron's came along and Vaux Breweries. Customers would be the ones really who decided after all. If they did not like the products, they would not buy it.

Changes over the years caused the breweries to have name changes–from Newcastle Breweries to Scottish and Newcastle breweries then to Scottish Courage, but now they are called Heineken North East.

Anyway, getting back to the earlier days, the breweries were quite generous with their hospitality. What I mean by that is, I would get a regular invite to St James' Park to watch Newcastle United play. Sometimes, we would go to the hospitality suite at the Brewery where they would allow you to sample their wares as some would say. There was a bar in the grounds of the brewery where we would go before a home game at St James' Park. Food and drink, courtesy of the brewery. We could then walk over to the football ground and watch the game, in a seat paid for by the brewery.

On a special occasion we could go into the brewery's box which overlooked the football pitch. We were given a three course meal with drinks. At half time, there would be refreshments and cakes. Other occasions were the Gosforth Park races on Northumberland Plate Day, the breweries would have a marquee with chandeliers, TV screens and a tote (book maker) and of course a bar. Once again, three course meals with all the trimmings. Days out on the golf course was another.

I did change breweries on several occasions as other brewers were in competition with each other. I would be offered a bit more discount on my purchase of beer.

Vaux Brewery were a Sunderland-based brewery. They also welcomed you to their hospitality suite, but what I really did like about Vaux was, at the actual brewery, they had horses and stables. The horses would deliver the beer to the pubs and bars around Sunderland town itself. The horses were magnificent and they were named after all the beers and lagers they produced. Such as Samson, Lorrimer, Labbatt, Tuborg.

The Vaux Brewery, like a lot of businesses can go through tough times and it is a shame that the brewery had to close.

Believe it or not, I also put Cameron's brewery products in the bar. This was before the original Lion brewery closed.

I was allowed to do those changes because I was a 'free trade' pub. This means that, unlike most pubs today, I was not renting the pub from the brewery.

Most of the time, if I got an invite to watch the game at Newcastle, I would take another person. I tried to make it fair by taking a different person each time. One time I remember taking Dave Nixon. This is the guy who would set his hair on fire, remember! He was a massive Newcastle United supporter.

I told him that he had to get dressed, not in his usual tracksuit and trainers, but shoes, pants and a shirt. I went to seek Dave this particular Saturday. I remember Newcastle United were playing Middlesbrough. He was dressed accordingly and we set off for the game. I told him to behave when we got there and lo and behold, he was on his best behaviour.

We went to the Hospitality Suite at the brewery. Even though he liked a pint or two, he didn't drink much. We had a good talk to everyone and we even played a quiz game where everyone was included. We didn't win but we were either second or third. The buffet was fabulous, as usual, and we were all treated well by the staff at the brewery.

Off we went to the game and we found our seats. The atmosphere was electric and everyone was having a good time.

Half time came around and people left their seats for a coffee or something to eat. Well, to my amazement, there was Dave Nixon sitting in his seat, munching away on a chicken drumstick. "Where did you get that from?" I asked. "I've got more in my Barbour jacket pockets if you want one?" he said. He then put his hand in his pocket and pulled out a chicken drumstick, covered in pieces of tobacco and other disgusting bits and bobs. He then did his best to dust it down before handing it towards me! "No thanks!" I said. He chuckled, and ate it himself.

He must have filled his pockets at the buffet earlier.

It's funny because when we arrived, I could see people looking at him quite sheepishly. He looked like the 'wild man from Borneo'. But by the time the second half of the game had started, he had an audience around him laughing and warming to his strange humour and behaviour.

Chapter 21
Bees

It was a sunny Saturday morning and we were just about to open the doors when I was asked by Ann to go into the rear yard area.

The yard was an area with picnic benches and people would sit out and have lunch or a drink in the sun. There were hanging baskets all around and the flowers were starting to look nice.

Getting back to me being asked to go outside… to witness a swarm of bees circling the whole of the yard. This looked like a dark cloud moving around the yard. This lasted for about five minutes then they all seemed to want to land on one of the hanging baskets. Within minutes, there were hundreds of bees landing on the underside of a hanging basket. Fascinated by this, I went and got my video camera and started to record. We opened the door to the public but we told them to not go into the back yard because of what was happening. The Queen bee was thrown out of the hive and was replaced by a younger Queen bee.

After a few phone calls, we managed to get in touch with a beekeeper, a young man who was starting out his own bee collection.

When he turned up, he put on his protective clothing, large hat with a net to protect his face. A large pair of gloves which went past his elbows, then he was ready. He had a large box with a sliding lid to collect the bees. With him was an old gentleman, probably in his late 70s, who used to be a beekeeper. This gentleman did not have any protective clothing.

The young chap had some sort of a smoke gun to smoke the bees. This made them drowsy. The bees all surrounded their Queen to protect her, but what the beekeeper had to do then was put his hands (with gloves) into the bees and find the Queen then push them down into the box and close the lid. Simple!… This chap had a few attempts but could not find the Queen. To my amazement, the old chap stepped in and took over. He calmly walked over to the young lad and told him to get the box ready. He then, with no protection on, put both hands in amongst the bees and bang! He pushed the bees into the box. It sounded like a brick had fallen into the box. He had successfully got the Queen and most of her followers into the box.

They then left the sliding lid open a little so that the other bees who were circulating the yard could go in and protect the Queen.

There was a small crowd of people watching by this time, as all in all, the beekeeper would have been there a couple of hours or so.

When they thought that they had most of the bees, they set off to give the bees their new home.

I remember talking to the older gentleman after he had dropped the bees into the box. He was a very interesting man. He had been keeping bees for years and he must have been stung hundreds of times. He just became immune to the feeling.

Chapter 22
Manager

Every business needs to have a good manager. Well I had just that. It was around 1989 and I found that I needed another member of bar staff, so I advertised.

I was working behind the bar one lunchtime and a young man came in and requested to put his name forward for the position of bar staff. He said he didn't have much time to stay and talk because he was working in another pub nearby, in the town of Morpeth and he was only on his lunch break.

He was well presented and spoke well. I asked him to come in for an interview and asked when he was available to start.

To cut a long story short, he was part of the team in no time. Paul Gray was his name and Paul seemed to fit straight in and his experience of working in the pub trade was valuable. Paul soon showed his capability and was working as a supervisor in no time.

Over the next few years we became very good friends. In 1995 I had purchased the old Co-op dairy which was next door to Bubbles. I quickly found myself too involved with the renovation and I was struggling to fit time into working in the bar.

Paul was managing Bubbles and he had taken over all of the management duties for running the pub.

I had earlier been to the Technical College and taken a course called The British Institute of Innkeeping.

Paul and a number of staff went to the local college and also took the course for the bar trade. This was a licensed trade diploma. It was invaluable as it covered all aspects of the licensed trade.

Anyway, getting back to Paul, I gave him the position of manager in Bubbles and then eventually, The Black Diamond.

Between the two pubs, we had a team of fifty staff who worked shifts starting at 6am and until closing at around 3am (at weekends).

A good manager and good team of supervisors and staff is the key to a good business.

Paul worked Monday to Fridays and took control of everything. I would work Saturdays and Sundays and most nights.

This worked well for many years.

When the time came in 2006 and I decided that I had had enough and wanted to sell both pubs, my main concern was Paul.

As we got nearer to the sell date, I heard that there could be an opportunity for a manager/steward in a nearby golf club. Paul said that he didn't want to stay at The Black Diamond under the new management.

I mentioned this to Paul and told him to go and leave his name. He did this and he was soon asked to go for an interview. After a second interview, Paul was offered the job. Great, I was pleased he was sorted.

Paul started his new job in May 2007.

I sold the pubs in October 2007. I had almost six months to get back involved full time.

Paul had been a good friend and manager to me. He was an honest and trustworthy person and we are still good friends today.

Chapter 23
Heroes

When people are asked about their heroes, they will probably say "Mike Tyson" or "Alan Shearer".

Well. One of my heroes is David Grieves. Who is David Grieves? Well David was a local lad from Ashington. He was born in 1959 with a heart defect, a valve missing in his heart. His parents were told that he would have a short life because of this, and from the day David was born he was going back and forth to hospital for most of his life.

He was a special lad who only wanted to do the things normal kids did like play football or run down the street or do the stuff normal kids could do.

I remember being at the Hirst South Junior School in Ashington. I must have been around ten years old. I remember being a 'Porch Monitor' at school. This was a privilege at the time as I was in charge of the porch. Me and another lad were there to make sure that kids didn't hang about or cause mischief. We would be in the porch at play times and at dinner time.

We had to keep an eye on a young lad called David. David was two years younger than me. He was quiet and never spoke, he just sat in the porch. I asked him why he was not out playing in the yard with all the other boys.

This was a school where the boys and girls were separated before comprehensive schools were introduced.

Getting back to David, he replied, "I'm not allowed to play with others in case I fall down or get hurt in any way." He explained about his condition the best he could at that age.

That was the first I saw of David Grieves.

I moved onto the 'Secondary Modern' school next, as I failed my eleven plus. I was never interested at school.

Two years later, David came into the same school–Hirst Park Secondary Modern Boys School. I was there for four years and left in 1972.

As it happens, after leaving school I saw David on the odd occasion and over the years we became very good friends.

David worked for a company called Remploy for most of his adult life. This was a company that specialised in special needs. Eventually, after many years he left Remploy.

David wanted to work in Bubbles. I employed him as bar staff and he ended up as supervisor.

He was quite an intelligent lad but he struggled a lot with his health. He was often ill with a cold or something or other, but he was always determined to fight it off. David was always in Bubbles either in or out of work.

During his life he kept on breaking through barriers. His parents were told he would not reach the age of ten. Then it extended from sixteen to twenty. He kept on breaking down these barriers with such a positive attitude.

At the age of thirty-eight, David's health deteriorated to such an extent that he only had a year or so to live. He was more constantly in and out of hospital.

He was offered the opportunity of going onto a shortlist of people who could receive a heart or even in his case a heart and lung transplant.

With no hesitation, David put his name forward.

During the next two years his health was really showing problems. David had a pager on him all the time to notify him when an opportunity arose for a transplant. He was always on guard.

I can't imagine what this must have felt like. Living each day like it could be your last.

We sat together in Bubbles one evening talking about what he had to do if his pager went off.

We also talked about what he wanted to do if he were to have a transplant.

He wanted, more than anything, just to be able to run the full length of his street. Something so mundane to many, but to him it meant the world. He went on to say how he wanted to go to the 'Transplant Games'.

Days after this conversation, miraculously his pager went off. The look of fear on my face, but Dave took it in his stride and said, "I'm away to get my new heart now" with a huge beam on his face.

We later found that the heart was not a match and he was sent home.

This happened again and David went back into the hospital. Once again, not a match.

Another evening, David was in Bubbles looking terrible. His health was showing its severity by now. His pager went off! He slowly took it out of his pocket and just said "Third time lucky, eh?". Off he went.

This time, a perfect match. David had the operation at the Freeman Hospital in Newcastle. It was a success.

He came out of hospital shortly after the transplant and went to stay with his brother, Barry.

I went to see David at his brother's house. I had to stay away from him in case of any infections but for the very first time, I noticed how blue his eyes were. I looked at him and thought to myself how good he looked. His eyes were bright blue and the purple tint to his lips had gone. David had the biggest smile I have ever seen.

He was now more determined to do what he wanted. Over the next few years, David progressed and he entered the transplant games. He went out walking and cycling as much as he could. He now had a life that was worth living and he was sure giving it his best shot. But David was told his new heart would not last forever.

In fact, he was told it would only give him a few extra years, but he was so grateful.

I remember David telling me that he held the record for being the quickest person to leave the hospital after a transplant.

He was forty years old, he had about five or six good years, then he became ill. His positive attitude kept him going and he knew how strong he was, constantly telling us how he was the only one left alive compared with all the others who were in for transplants at the same time. David was determined to reach his fiftieth birthday. He had so far broken all the records he had set.

He had his fiftieth birthday on 8th May, 2009.

David died in July, 2009.

Chapter 24
Makis–the Greek lad

One summer, I went to Greece with the lads. Fenwick, Alan and John. We were away for two weeks. We had a brilliant time, most of the evenings would be spent in the local bars. We met a guy in one bar who was the bar man and we got on great.

One evening we were out and we had a pint or two. We were with Makis the barman in his bar. It was late and the music had to stop before the police did their rounds to make sure that there was no loud noise.

One night in particular, we were having a cracking night and good laugh when the police walked in. Fenwick was the loudest, and he didn't laugh, he screamed. The police asked Fenwick why he was screaming, but he replied, "It's because I'm drunk, I always scream when I'm drunk." The police had a quiet word with Makis and off they went.

We walked past the bar the next day and noticed a letter on the door written in Greek. There was Makis sitting in the bar adjacent. We went over to him, asked what was going on and he explained that the police had forced him to shut for two weeks because they reported somebody screaming.

Later in the holiday, I had been out to the shops. I returned to my hotel room to find the lads sitting on my bed with Makis. "We have just interviewed Makis and we have mutually appointed him as the new barman in Bubbles," they explained.

Makis came over to England at the end of his season in Kos. He came and lived with me at my house in North Seaton Road and during his time working for me, he helped me develop the best cocktail menu in town.

Originally, we planned for him to stay for only a couple of weeks. However, the passport office kept his passport on his entry into England and they said they would post it to my house.

But the passport office had lost his passport!

Three months later after numerous phone calls, his passport arrived at my house and off he went back to Greece.

Another incompetent department in our wonderful country!

Chapter 25
Beer Festivals

Shortly after opening Bubbles, Cask conditioned beers were becoming popular. CAMRA were becoming a talking point. Real Ale was put on the bar and became a good seller. It brought a good customer into the bar. It also had regular beer drinkers trying it.

I decided to have a Beer Festival in Bubbles. No other bar in town had done it before, so now was a good time. I got a load of scaffolding set up where the stage area was and ordered twenty-six different ales and ciders. The beers and ciders had to be put on the scaffold and tapped and spilled.

Real ales then had hops in the casks and shouldn't be moved once opened otherwise the sediment would rise up and disperse in the beer.

Another thing with real

Ron Storey–supervisor and Paul Gray–Manager

ales is once the cask has been tapped and spilled, air gets into the cask and the beer starts to turn. The average life of a real cask ale is about five days. The stronger the beer, the longer it will last. Eighteen casks of beer and cider to sell in one week. It was difficult to say the least.

I had a couple more beer festivals, then the trend died off a little.

Chapter 26
Stars in their eyes

M any a night would go by and I would be trying to think of new ideas to bring a bit of money into the bar.

Unplugged, at this time it must have been around 1989. Nobody was hosting live buskers' nights or unplugged sessions.

On a Sunday evening, I would have the stage set up with a drum kit, lead guitar, bass guitar, acoustic guitar and microphones. Anyone could get up and we had some great times.

Another idea was on a Sunday evening after unplugged days had run their toll. Karaoke was the 'in thing'. I wanted to spruce it up a bit, so I came up with the idea of having a prize of up for £100. The winner would have to dress and sound like someone famous. Stars in your eyes was a popular TV show at the time, so why not change the name for copyright and have our own version. Stars in 'their' eyes.

I put an advertisement in the free paper and it said something like this: Stars in their eyes, karaoke competition. Come along to sing and dress like your favourite artist and you could win £100.

All entries had to be genuine to make it work so I said that any applicant had to call in at Bubbles to pick up an entry form and pay £5.00. This £5.00 would be returned to all entries when they turned up on the night of the competition.

We needed six entries to hold a show and within the first week we had the six. We also had a list of people who wanted to enter if anyone dropped out, which never happened.

The interest was unbelievable. The whole town was talking about it.

People thought that Matthew Kelly, the man on the telly, was coming to Bubbles.

On the night, Bubbles was all set up. We had stars hanging from the ceiling, curtains on the front of the stage and the smoke machine out.

I asked the council if they could help with judging as I needed a non-biased judge. They obliged and said they would send the Civic Head as it is one of their duties.

That was it. Everything in place and the show was on.

The Civic Head turned up with his wife and they brought the Lord Mayor of Durham. I still wonder if they too also thought Matthew Kelly was coming.

I set out four judges' chairs in the front of the stage. I told the staff to give the Civic Head and his company a couple of complimentary drinks for their services.

The doors were opened and within minutes, the bar was packed.

The show was a huge success and everything went to plan.

I believe the winner on the night was a young lady who impersonated Natalie Imbruglia. She pipped at the post a gentleman who had been on the actual TV show, singing as Bing Crosby.

A great night had by all. Well when I say all. I found out that the Civic Head and his company had almost drunk the bar dry. Their bill was into the hundreds. This chap, the Civic Head, not mentioning any names, was getting drinks for all the females in the bar, assuming they were on the house.

There's always someone, isn't there?

Chapter 27
Bank Holidays

Bank holiday Mondays were a busy time in Bubbles. It started off by putting bands on during the afternoon and evening. August bank holidays were the first.

A friend had died of leukaemia and I wanted to raise money for the charity.

I managed to get thirteen bands to come into Bubbles and play free of charge.

It was a crazy day as you can imagine, very successful and we raised a lot of money and sent it off to the charity.

After a couple of years doing the August bank holiday, the interest of both customers having a good time and bands wanting to play, I decided to do all bank holidays. I reduced the bands to six, then eventually to four.

They were great days, people could come and enjoy the day and best of all, there was no trouble. What I found was the customers who enjoyed their live music were decent people.

I would have to go up to Bubbles early in the morning, set up a drum kit for all band drummers to use and the kit had to be miked up.

Trevor Wharton was the engineer/DJ at the time and was always known as Dr Trevor. He could fix anything electrical. He also had a small recording studio at his home.

Many local bands would send their broken amplifiers and mixing desks and speakers to Trevor to be repaired. He specialised in old "valve amps". These were guitar amplifiers which had the old valves inside and were particularly difficult to repair, or so I'm told.

There was one bank holiday in particular, that I remember in August 1999. As usual, I was in Bubbles early setting up the drum kit with Trevor who had brought his large mixing desk and we were doing a sound check for the PA system. My mother and stepdad Ken came into the pub with my daughter Rebecca.

Rebecca had just turned three years old the month previous. Rebecca had not seen anything like this before and she was fascinated. She could not understand how the sound would come out of the PA speakers when you spoke down the microphone.

Rebecca was a happy child and was always singing. I showed her how to use the microphone and I laid it down on the stool. I could see the fascination in her eyes and I knew it would not take long before she would pick it up.

I went over to Trevor who was behind his mixing desk and I asked if he could put together a tape of her singing, but don't let her see you otherwise she will stop. It didn't take long before we got a rendition of Rudolph the red nose reindeer in the middle of summer.

My daughters Jenny (above)
and Rebecca

Trevor took the tape away and mixed it into a CD. This was played every Christmas in Bubbles.

The years that followed, both Rebecca and Jenny, my two daughters, would come into Bubbles on a bank holiday and would sit and play on the drums and have a go on the mixing desk before we opened the doors to the public.

Happy days.

Chapter 28
Birthday Sing-a-gram

It was Sunday night and it was March 29th, my birthday. I can't remember what year. I was at work and the bar had been busy for a couple of hours. It was packed. It was around 9pm when all of a sudden a scantily dressed girl appeared behind the bar with suspenders, bra and high heels. She was a pretty girl and blessed in the bra area! The whole pub fell deadly silent. The music was turned off and the girl walked towards me singing" Happy Birthday".

My girlfriend Ann and the rest of the staff had arranged a sing-a-gram.

The whole thing was over in five minutes. As she left, I noticed a friend of mine, Roy Fox, was standing in the crowd smiling. Strange, I thought, what's he smiling at? He had a combat-style jacket on and a pair of trainers. That was it. He proceeded to walk around the bar with no trousers on. No one noticed. He then disappeared, returning with trousers on. Nobody batted an eyelid.

On a night out with my brother and his then partner, we were in Newcastle. We had a good night, visiting a few pubs along the quayside. We even ended up in some nightclub, not my scene. We ended the night with a visit to the Indian restaurant and we had a great night.

At the end of our meal, we were finishing off our drinks, when two men sat at a table next to us. It looked like they had just finished work, possibly Doormen. They were heavily built lads all dressed in black, wearing the then typical Crombie coat attire of Doormen. It didn't take long before my brother Paul said to one of the men, "Do you mind, that's my girlfriend you are talking about!" I didn't hear what was discussed between the lads, but I knew it must have been something derogative for Paul to say something, Paul typically being a quiet lad. The two men continued to be sleazy and suggestive towards Paul's girlfriend. Paul knew it was wise to leave, so he went to pay the bill. Next thing I know, the two men stood up just as their meal was being served. A few heated words were exchanged before one of the men walked towards my brother. I got up from my chair and went to stand between them, putting my arm in front of my brother. I tried to diffuse the situation by telling Paul not to get involved. Just as the words came out of my mouth the second man ran over and lunged toward me screaming "what are you going to do about it, you old git!".

The next thing I know, he had landed in his vindaloo. I pushed my brother towards the door to get away.

We walked out of the restaurant and onto the street. The two men decided to follow and were shouting abuse at us, looking to start trouble. We continued to ignore them and walk away but noticed that they increased their speed, trying their best to catch us up. I will never forget the smell of that vindaloo.

I knew trouble was about to catch us up and I turned to my brother and said, "Well that's it, we will have to give it our best shot, we have no other choice if they go for us."

The threats from behind continued so I stopped and turned around to confront the two men. Then suddenly one of them jumped into the middle of the road right in front of a passing car. He had lost it! he started to bang on the bonnet of the car, screaming for the car to stop. The driver got out of the car and the next thing I knew, I was grabbed from behind. I didn't know who it was. They had one arm around my neck and were trying to pull me back over onto the floor. I dropped to my knees, managing to pull the person over my shoulder.

To my amazement I saw a policeman's helmet rolling on the ground and a chap dressed in uniform sprawled on the ground before me. "Shit!" I thought. Then all of a sudden, I was jumped on by more police, handcuffed and put into the back of a police car.

Next thing I knew, I had arrived at the police station.

I was put on bail and let out at 4am to find Paul in the station waiting for me. "What the hell happened?" I said to him.

Well, this is where it gets interesting. The arresting officer was a young lady, who believe it or not, was a regular customer in Bubbles and The Black Diamond. The weeks following were rather strange to say the least.

This young female officer, whom I have chosen to keep anonymous, would come into my bars with her friends. She had been overheard one evening whilst on a social night out that she was 'keeping an eye on this place… and if there's anything not right it's getting reported'. She attended the pub on a couple of occasions and was seen and heard by staff.

I had no choice but to tell the Doormen working for me at Bubbles that she was no longer welcome and to refuse her entry. This is avoiding the fact that she breached her position by attending a pub knowing the situation.

The next thing I know, she was sat in The Black Diamond staring at me while I worked. She was politely asked to leave.

Within a few days I got a call from the police, about the female officer. He discussed the situation and accused me of barring the young lady mentioned because of her position as a police officer. "Rubbish," I replied. "I have told her to stay away until my court case is over and she should know this anyway."

A few months went by and I appeared in the court at Newcastle Police Station, how convenient eh? My trial went ahead and witnesses from both sides were called, including this young police officer. I listened, and thought to myself what a load of rubbish. I said my piece and was followed by my solicitor, who was only young at the time but she was fantastic. She had done all her research and discovered that the guy who originally started the brawl back in the Indian restaurant had a police record. He was on the sex offenders register. He had been to court on a number of occasions relating to this. I was instantly acquitted.

The arresting officer stormed out of the court room, witnessed by all.

Chapter 29
Iolanda

During our lifetime we all meet all sorts of people from different backgrounds.

In the early days before Bubbles, my girlfriend Ann worked for a local dentist in Ashington called McMeekin's Dentist. She went to work there straight from school as a dental nurse.

Over the years, Mr McMeekin became a very close friend as well as Ann's boss. He was from a good background, well educated and lived in Gosforth. He would have clients who were well off, to say the least.

One of these clients was a lady called Iolanda Gibbins. She was the wife of Mr Gibbins of Adams and Gibbons in the motor trade. Mr Gibbons had passed years before we got to know Iolanda.

She lived in the manor house at Cresswell and she was a very wealthy lady.

Over the years, she became very close to Ann. I was introduced to her company.

We would on the odd occasion have a drive down to Cresswell for a drink and a chat or to go out for a meal.

When we opened Bubbles, we served food which was cooked in a very small kitchen. Ann would occasionally bake a quiche or make a lasagne and take it down to the manor house for Iolanda. Simple food, cooked well. "Home cooking" Iolanda would call it and she loved it.

I remember on one occasion Ann said that Iolanda wanted to come to Bubbles for lunch. We wanted to impress her, so we set out a small table for her and decorated the table. She arrived and enjoyed her lunch.

We had a good lunchtime trade, serving a small selection of food. It is strange what can happen and how it's good to know people who are in the right place.

A strange thing happened one year when Ann was learning to drive and she decided to buy a small car, an Austin Metro. Being the people we are, we like to support the business of the people we know. So Ann decided to look at cars at Adams and Gibbons car showroom where there was a Mini Metro.

She purchased the car and took driving lessons.

The day of her test, the examiner got into her car, got straight back out and said, "I cannot do your test in that car, it's unsafe". In her horror Ann said she had just bought it from a garage. The examiner told her to take it straight back.

Ann was in tears.

A good friend of ours who owned his own garage, Geoff Middleton, who was a mechanical engineer, checked the car over and said that the chassis was twisted. It looked as if the car had been in an accident. He said he would come to the garage we had bought it from as a witness.

Off we went to the Adams and Gibbons garage. Ann, myself and Geoff.

On arrival at the garage, I asked for the manager. This chap came through to see us as we were standing in the garage. I told him the problem, but he seemed unscathed by this and he said there was nothing he could do. I told him we didn't want the car and we wanted our money back. This was all said in the workshop of the garage in front of the mechanics.

The conversation got heated and he was adamant that there was nothing wrong with the car. Well, I'm not usually one for name dropping but I thought this was the perfect circumstance to do so. As we turned to walk away, I calmly said, "You'll be lucky if you are working here tomorrow. We are good friends with Iolanda Gibbons and because of your attitude you will be reported to her." He stood with a smirk on his face but also I could see that hint of blankness–who is Iolanda Gibbons? he was probably thinking.

We left the garage and set off to open Bubbles for the evening. We discussed whether or not we should talk to Iolanda. Rushing back, we got to Bubbles just before 6pm and I went straight into the pub to hear the phone ringing. It was the manager from the car garage, trying to offer me another car. He was desperate for me to take the offer. Looks like he did his research on who Iolanda Gibbons was! We went to the garage the next day and he presented us with a lovely little Mini Metro. We took the car and the rest was history.

We never mentioned it to Iolanda.

Chapter 30
Ski Accident

1990, February.

A new ski resort was open in Scotland. The resort was a place called Aonach Mor. This was an area in the mountains next to Ben Nevis. The resort opened in 1989. I had been to Scotland several times, resorts such as Glencoe and Glenshee.

I went for a weekend skiing with Paul Gray and Bill Sephton.

We had a bad drive up as the weather was poor, wind and rain all the way.

There was a close incident, when a tree was blown over on the road in front of us only seconds before.

We arrived in Fort William at our hotel, which from what I remember was nice.

We had a couple of drinks in the bar and headed down into the town for a couple more.

There was plenty of snow and it was cold. The forecast for the following days was a good one, meaning, cold and plenty of snow.

Sure enough, the next morning we set off for the slopes, only to find that my brakes had frozen on the car and it took a while to free them.

On the slopes we had a good day, plenty of snow.

We awoke the next day to find it had 'dumped it down', snowed all night. The slopes were covered, in fact, when we got there, the piste machine had not been over all the ski slopes. Some of the lower slopes were untouched. "Great," I thought as previous years when I had been away, I had tried 'off-piste skiing'. It is different to skiing 'on the piste' where the machine has compressed and smoothed out the snow.

There were queues to go to the top slopes where the machine had been, and just to mention, the top slopes had been closed the day before, due to high winds.

Perfect, no one on the lower slopes and lovely deep virgin snow.

I went to the second level, where I had skied the day before and off I went.

It was fantastic, the conditions were great and nice deep snow. I made about five or six turns, traversing down the slope, when all of a sudden, I remember seeing something out of the corner of my eye. Someone had set themselves away down from the top slopes where the piste machine had been, they then arrived on the lower slopes where the piste machine had not been. I don't know what happened, but I presume that they had maybe not skied off-piste before?

That was it.

I remember lying down the side of the mountain amongst the rocks with a ski guide next to me. He had put a blanket over me and was talking to me. Everything was red? My eyes must have been bloodshot or something, I thought, when all of a sudden I started to vomit. All the snow around me was covered in blood.

I passed out, then awoke in the cable car, strapped to a stretcher, looking out of the window and I remember the chap pointing and saying "That's where you fell". I passed out again, only to wake being hurried into an ambulance at the bottom of the ski slopes. Then again passing out and going into, then out of, a hospital in Fort William.

I was then rushed over some tarmac to be put into a helicopter.

In and out of consciousness, I was sent to Southern General Neurological Hospital in Glasgow.

I had been knocked off the ski slope and ended up with five fractures to the right side of my head. A broken bone in my ear which has caused my deafness, dislodged my inner ear which affected my balance.

Not bad eh… Apart from that, I was ok?!

I would like to give my sincere thanks to all the staff at the Southern General Hospital in Glasgow, for their kind help at that time.

Chapter 31
Bubbles trip to Amsterdam

On one occasion we decided to have a trip to Amsterdam. I put a list up in Bubbles and asked if anyone was interested in going to Amsterdam. Within a week or so we had a dozen or so names of interested people. All lads of course. We booked our travel, which was two nights on the North Sea Ferry. My father had never been abroad so at the tender age of sixty he got his first passport and off we went.

The bus trip down to the ferry at that time was in Harwich, was about eight hours or so then onto the ferry we went. Geordie, my dad, was very nervous. It was a strange experience for him going to a foreign country. No sooner had we got aboard the ferry, he was in the shop buying a litre bottle of rum.

One of the lads, Fenwick, had paid for a cabin whereas the rest of us decided to sleep in chairs. We all went into the bar where there was a disco. We were all in high spirits. As the night went on into the early hours of the morning, we were all getting a bit tired and I noticed my dad was sitting at a table fast asleep. He had finished off his full bottle of rum. We all tried to wake him but to no avail. We decided to take him to Fenwick's cabin and put him to bed. Back to the disco we all went. As we arrived, we had not been there more than five minutes when a fight broke out. There were glasses and punches being thrown. The roller shutters came down at the bar. I noticed to the side of me one of the guys 'Seph', a bit of a joker, was trying to crawl under the shutters shouting "Excuse me, please can I have another pint!" We had nothing to do with the trouble, so it was an earlier than we'd imagined end to the night.

There were five of us who ended up in the cabin: Kevin was sleeping with my father, Tom (Ann's Dad) was in the other bed and myself and Alan were on the floor. No sign of Fenwick yet he was the one who had booked the room for himself.

Early the next morning I heard a few moans and groans then suddenly a voice "Giss a kiss". Shouts and screams came from my father who had woken up to find Kevin in bed with him asking him for a kiss. (Nothing in it by the way.)

Next thing is Geordie went into the shower to try and sober up. He was naked when he switched on the shower and screams of what sounded like agony came from the bathroom. The water was freezing.

After a tour of the 'clog' factory, then the 'cheese factory' and finished off with the 'delft' factory, we ended up in Amsterdam city centre. The bus driver warned us that the bus would leave at 4pm and not to be late.

That was it, let's explore. We all went for some food in McDonald's then for a wander through the red light district. It didn't take us long to find it.

We were all in a pub on a corner of the street. Fenwick laughed and said look at this, and we all shuffled to the window. "Watch this guy," Fenwick said. There was a chap wanting to spend a few quid. He was walking past a young girl who was sitting in a window. He went past a couple of times, then he went to the door and opened it, spoke to the girl then came back out and walked away. Not too far, may I add.

He quickly went through the money in his pocket and returned to the room and went in. "Right," said Fenwick. "I'm going to time him", looking at his watch. Five minutes later the guy came out and we all stood there laughing and banging on the windows and pointing to our watches.

He didn't hang around too long.

We all had a few beers then we ventured down the street, window shopping. Tom said to the lads, "Why don't we all chip in for Geordie, we will get him a nice one." The look of embarrassment on Geordie's face was a picture. Before we knew it, it was nearly 4pm and we all scurried back to the bus. The return journey on the ferry was a quieter one and we were home before we knew it.

Chapter 32
2006

It was now early 2006. I was at the stage in my life where I was thinking "Is there more to life than this?". I was 49 years old and the pub trade was tiring. There were constant problems, which would never go away because of customers and staff. There were now fifty staff between the two pubs who worked between them from 6am until 3am. I thought to myself, it's time to go. I will get the two pubs valued and I will put them up for sale. I did just that and by February 2006 both Bubbles and The Black Diamond Inn were on the market.

The first year was difficult, one person then another would come and have a look but to be honest, I think the business was too big for the average buyer.

I was asked to sell them separately, but I said no. They were to be sold as a pair. I did not want to be left with one and have someone next door in competition with me.

A year passed by and I got a call from the agent who was selling the business. He said he had an interested party who was Cameron's Leisure, a company who had just reformed after closing down. They were a Hartlepool company and they were buying ready made businesses and putting them up for tenancy. Great news, I thought. Cameron's were very interested in buying and things seemed fine at the beginning.

"Be prepared to be out within four weeks," they told me. This should give me enough time to run down my stock as they did not want any of it.

The next four weeks were anxious. I told all of my staff and we started to run down all of the stock. Four weeks came and went with no completion date in sight. Maybe next week?

I ended up having to order more stock to keep the pubs open, you can't have a pub with no beer.

The same happened again the following week.

This went on from February throughout the spring, then over the summer and into autumn. I had begun to have had enough. My business was beginning to struggle and things were just not looking good.

I rang the agent on a Wednesday and I had a long conversation, but I felt I was being told the same story again and again. "I have had enough," I said. "I will give you and the buyer until Friday to sort this out otherwise the deal is off!" They told me I couldn't do that; the agent said, "I have invested too much money and time for you to do that." I was adamant, though. "Well sort it out, or believe me I will call the whole deal off and I will build up the trade and sell in a year or two with another agent," was my reply.

Friday came and I got a phone call around 4pm. "Can we wait until Monday?" said the agent. "Cameron's are having an emergency meeting then." "I am not playing silly games. They either want it or they don't," I said. But I agreed to wait until Monday. Monday came and went with a barrage of excuses. Then Tuesday, then Wednesday.

I was beginning to think that the deal was not going to happen and started to prepare myself mentally for the end result.

At around 4pm on the Wednesday I got a phone call from my solicitor and he said that he had received a payment from Cameron's but it was £50k short. "What do you want me to do?" he asked.

"Keep the money they have sent and tell them the deal is off until the full amount is paid," I said hastily.

The excitement I was witnessing was unbelievable. The deal was going through and my solicitor had the majority of the money. I could hardly believe it. I was finally on the brink of selling.

The telephone rang around half an hour later and my solicitor said, "They have paid off the rest of the money."

"Bloody hell, what do I do now?" I asked. "Nothing but hand the keys over to the staff and walk away," he said.

What…?

This was an unreal thing to do. All the years of hard work, then within a split second… walk away.

A local lad and his wife were to take over a new tenancy agreement with Cameron's but they were on holiday. I said I would be there to help until they came back, around a week later.

The staff were quite capable of running the business, so I told them to call if they needed me.

They never called. That was it.

I was now unemployed. I went into the pubs when the new tenants returned from their holiday. They were now the new owners of the business.

They continued to put on local bands and continued to play live music in Bubbles.

Neil Brannaghan and his partner Michelle were now the owners of the two businesses.

Neil was a musician himself and a very good one I may add and his ambition to put bands in Bubbles was inspiring.

Chapter 33
Religion and me

Well, even though I believed from an early age, especially with the experiences that I have witnessed over the years, my belief is that religion took a change in direction.

Being in the bar trade is a way of life, and sometimes it gets in the way of normal everyday activities which I would say that normal people do. Working ridiculous hours both early in the morning and late at night causes problems at home. What I want to touch upon is my personal experience.

I met my girlfriend Ann when I was sixteen years old. We were courting for around twenty-three years. We got married in 1996. This is at the time we were building The Black Diamond Inn.

I had my own house before we were married and Ann moved in with me.

Over the following years, I was hardly at home when building The Black Diamond Inn and working in the two bars. During which time I gained a night club licence for Bubbles. This gave me an opportunity to expand the business a bit more. Looking back I do feel that the real heart of Bubbles was taken away with the night club. But nevertheless, it is all about finding ways of surviving in this world.

Long days and longer nights, I was never at home. My early years of marriage were almost non-existent. This led to problems at home and I started to feel I was better off at work. I enjoyed the company of staff and friends more than going home. Obviously this caused many disagreements.

Apparently, there are more disagreements in the bar trade than any other employment. I read that somewhere, and I do believe it.

All of this led to me enjoying the company of friends more, one in particular, Leoni. This caused problems at home. By 2004, I was divorced.

Leoni came to live with me in 2011. She passed in 2012. My whole world fell apart and my belief in religion was now non-existent.

In my younger years, I must have been around seventeen years old, when I had a strange experience. I was living at home with my mother and my brother Paul.

My mother and father had been divorced a year earlier.

We moved to a council house in Green Lane in Ashington. This was the first house I had lived in as previously we were always in flats. I shared a large bedroom with my brother, which was sectioned off with a stud partitioned wall and arch doorway.

My brother was in bed; he was only six years old then.

When it was time for me to go to bed, my mother said, "Leave the stair head light on because Paul is not well and I am frightened he gets up and falls down the stairs through the night." This I did.

It lasted for a few nights, every night she said the same.

She would go to bed and turn the light off. She would call in and see to my brother before going to her room. She would also look into my room.

One night, I remember lying half asleep and I heard my mother walking up the stairs and walking towards our room. I had my back to her, so I tried to acknowledge her by turning around to see her.

Well what happened next was not my mother. It was my grandfather, my grandmother and Butch, the boxer dog. All standing in the doorway. I got such a fright that I turned away quickly, only to think what am I doing. I turned back around to see if they were still there. Luckily for me, no they were not. I got up and dashed downstairs and saw my mother watching TV. She jumped up. The look on my face must have been a picture. "What on earth is the matter?" she said. I sat down and told her of my experience.

We spent some time downstairs, scared to go back up. Eventually, the tiredness got the better of both of us.

She left the stair head light on all night, and the next few nights.

Things settled down and I soon forgot about my experience. We got back into our routine of leaving the stair head light on, my mother turning it off once she made her way to bed.

Well guess what, about a week later I turned around when I heard my mother walk into my room and there they were again, my grandmother, my grandfather and the dog. This time I had it in my head I was just imagining it and I tried to see it through. As

I stared at the shadowy figures, I saw my granddad smile at me and just as if they were made of smoke, they vanished. Again, I jumped out of bed and ran downstairs to see my mother sitting watching the TV. I sat and repeated the tale of the week before.

That was it for a while, until years later I was asked by Ann's mother to go to a spiritualist church with her. Obviously, I had told her my story many times.

Sheila, Ann's mother, was a spiritualist and so was Ann. The funny thing is, so was my mother. They were all christened through the Spiritualist Church.

Sheila was very interested in this and I went to church on several occasions with her.

On my first visit, I was given a message from an elderly lady whom I later become very good friends with. Her name was Mrs Munday and she was an acting spiritualist at the church who could give clairvoyance and clairaudience.

Towards the end of the church meeting, Mrs Munday looked at me and said, "I have your grandfather here and he is telling me that he gave you a fright one night. He tells me, however, you were not scared the second time he visited." Tears filled my eyes and I couldn't believe how accurate this was. I never had met Mrs Munday before.

This was the start of a long friendship with Mrs Munday.

Mrs Munday was in her 80s when I first met her. She was a small frail lady. Her door was always open. I was fascinated by her and the things she told me. She went into the depth of spiritualism.

I was later invited to join a developing circle at her home. This is where a small group of people act together, the circle number is seven. I sat within the circle for around two and a half years every Monday evening at 7.00pm. People came and went in our circle over time, but I only ever missed two weeks whilst on holiday. The whole idea is that you develop your psychic abilities as most people are supposed to have some thing or other. I used to think, watching some people entering the circle, how quick their psychic ability developed. They would start to see things (spirits) or hear something, seeing bodies that nobody else in the room could see. I had my doubts from the very start. I saw nothing, but I always felt great once I left the circle.

This all happened around 1982-1984. Then one night I was sitting in the circle and I felt different. I felt that I was being pulled over to the left then the right whilst still sitting straight upright on my chair. It felt like I was almost at right angles on the chair, but when I opened my eyes again, I had not moved.

Mrs Munday knew that I was being tested by the spirit. She said towards the end of the meeting that I was being tested. How did she know? I never mentioned a single thing to her about my experience.

This was the start for me. Over the next 3 months I had other weird experiences until one day Mrs Munday had come down with shingles and the circle had to stop.

She told me all about what was to come with Bubbles and the next business after Bubbles, The Black Diamond.

I used to call in and see if she was OK and she would always make me feel comfortable and put the kettle on for us both. Before

I knew it, she would be talking to someone else in the room, usually someone she described as her spirit guide.

A lot of the things she told me came true later in life.

I remember Mrs Munday one day, sitting having a cup of tea and chatting to me and she stopped, had a little mumble and then said to me "You will not believe this, I have just been told by my the spirit guide, I am not finished yet and that I will live to see my 100th birthday and letter from the Queen." I was puzzled at first, being in her mid-eighties, already frail and now ill with shingles it all just seemed very optimistic.

Mrs Munday died a few weeks after her 100th birthday and she did get her letter from the Queen.

I would go to church meetings all around the North East. I would go to churches where no one knew me and occasionally get messages from spirits. I believed in this and I respected the genuine people who practised the religion.

Chapter 34
The one percent

G etting back to Bubbles and the town of Ashington.
What I found by being in the bar trade was how different
people are. What I mean about that is, I call them the one percent.

Most of the people from Ashington are what I call the 'Salt of
the Earth'. Real, genuine people who are friendly, easy going and
kind.

Then there's the one percent. I suppose it's in towns all over the
world, but the few that walked through my doors seemed to only
want to cause trouble or fight. They had no respect. I won't go into
the nitty gritty, but I emphasised that my staff showed the utmost
respect to all of our customers. However, there would always be
the local idiot that would start disrespecting my staff, shouting and
throwing their weight about. The aim was to dissolve the situation
before it escalated by asking them to leave the bar. Often my duty
as the owner was to approach these folk and ask them to behave or
leave. Well as you can imagine, some of them would not like being
told and it occasionally ended in violence. This is where, as I said
earlier, my boxing came in handy. I can honestly say that I have

never started or caused any trouble in my life, I have only tried to diffuse or end trouble. But when you have someone throwing punches at you, of course you have self-defence.

Try telling this to the police. On many occasions, I have been arrested, sometimes at 3 or 4 o'clock in the morning because of some idiot causing trouble and ending up worse off.

I have always been a law-abiding person and never agreed with trouble.

In fact, I hate cruelty to animals. I believe in good manners and morals.

I have had many incidents where the police have intervened and I have been treated badly.

I have lost all faith and trust in the police and the legal system. I will leave it at that, because I could go on forever.

Chapter 35
Ashington hospital

One evening towards the end of the night around 11.00pm the telephone rang in Bubbles. It was the hospital asking if I could do them a favour. They had a medical emergency but had run out of ice. They asked if I could take any to them and I did so immediately. I locked up as quickly as I could, throwing money into the safe. I emptied the whole ice machine into carrier bags and rushed down to the hospital where I handed over bags of ice.

I found out later that they had a heart to be transported to the Freeman Hospital in Newcastle. Did I manage to save someone's life? Maybe.

On another occasion, one lunchtime in Bubbles, we were serving food and had our regular customers in. There was a family who came in, a mother, grandparents and grandson. They were sitting directly opposite the bar when Ann noticed the elderly gentleman didn't look too well. He was beginning to take a bad turn. Ann ran to the phone and called an ambulance. We rushed over to the man and tried to keep him calm until help arrived. The paramedics arrived and took control.

Apparently, he had suffered from a heart attack. Thanks to the quick thinking of Ann, the man survived.

A few weeks later he came into the bar and thanked us for saving his life.

We had another character called Mr Parr. An elderly man who came in every lunchtime with his dog Polly. We felt sorry for him as he was very frail and lived alone. He would walk into Bubbles every lunchtime and we would give him his lunch for free. This went on for years.

I remember one day we gave him ham and chips. He picked up the pieces of ham and said "What's this?" "Ham," I replied. "It's a bit thin, isn't it?" he said, seeming rather annoyed. He then proceeded to give the ham to his dog. That's gratitude for you. He never paid for a meal, yet he was not content. Nevertheless, he was back again the next day and we made sure he had something different to eat. He was happier.

Chapter 36
Crown Court

I have had many incidents in the bar where that 1% again cannot control their behaviour when they have had a drink or two. One of these incidents was a bank holiday. It was a Sunday and I had been working in The Black Diamond at lunchtime serving Sunday lunches as these were very popular. I would work from 8.00am until we finished serving lunch at around 5.00pm.

Then it was a bit of my time. I would unwind by having a drink with my mates who were also my customers in The Black Diamond. Then I would go over to Bubbles when it opened at 7.00pm.

This one particular night there were quite a few staff out celebrating the bank holiday and we were in Bubbles as a group. There was a karaoke on that evening and the bar was full. A good crowd were in and everyone was having a good time. One female member of staff was in my friendship group. She was sitting enjoying a drink after working her dayshift. Her boyfriend came in and didn't seem to like the fact that she was sitting in our company. He wanted her to leave and go home. She protested, saying she didn't want to go home and wanted to stay out a bit longer. He then got quite aggressive with her and grabbed her and started to pull her towards the door. She refused and an argument started between the two of them. Again, he tried to pull her to the door and she was holding a bottle from which she was drinking through a straw. She hit him over the head with the bottle. They were separated by customers who were standing nearby and he was pushed out.

The girl was then sitting on a bar stool, upset. A few minutes later, he came back in, walked up to her and punched her in the face. She fell to the floor and there was a group of lads who grabbed him and took him outside. A couple of members of staff rushed to attend to her, but she got up and ran after him.

During all of this, I was on the stage singing. I had no idea what was going on. I came off the stage after my song and went to the toilets. They were outside in the back yard.

On my return to the bar, one of my bar staff ran towards me in distress, telling me that the boyfriend was banging his girlfriend's head off the back gates. I remember hearing a couple of thuds in the back yard, I then ran outside. I witnessed with my own eyes as he grabbed her by her throat and dragged her up the back street.

I stood in the shadows and I thought I would watch what was happening and not rush over. They were arguing as he dragged her. I remember thinking to myself what to do? She is a member of my staff and is in a vulnerable situation. She was scared. I stayed hidden in the shadows and followed them up the lane watching him drag her then stop and argue on several occasions.

He then started to hit her. I came out of the shadows and shouted at him to stop. I walked towards the couple to make sure she was ok, but her boyfriend then took a swing at me in temper. As it happens, I tripped off the kerb and fell towards the ground. The boyfriend then threw a barrage of punches at me, luckily most of them missing me with a few just grazing the top of my head. I protected myself and managed to throw a good left hook, which caught him and threw him back from hitting me.

However, he came back again. I had managed to get to my feet and I was ready this time. My boxing kicked in and he ended up on the floor. I told the girl, a member of staff, to come back to Bubbles where she was safe until we could make sure she got home and away from her boyfriend. To my surprise she said "No" and that she wanted to stay with him. I was shocked, but said "Ok, if it is what you want". But I warned her that nobody could help her if she went home with him and he started again.

I then returned to Bubbles to be greeted by Trevor the DJ and a couple of staff. I told them what had happened. We were all concerned for our friend's safety.

However, the night continued and before we knew it, it was time to go home.

Later that night, I was lying in bed, only to be woken by someone banging on my door. The police had arrived. They had come to arrest me at 4.00am, regarding the altercation from earlier.

I was taken to the police station and put in a police cell for the night. They kept me there until around teatime the following day. A bank holiday Monday, when I had all the bands playing at Bubbles.

What followed made my beliefs in any police system reach a new low. I went to the county court on a couple of occasions. I was referred later to crown court.

During this time the police were prosecuting and I ended up in the crown court. I could not believe what lies and deception the police and their barrister had thrown at me!

I will leave out what happened in the crown court.

Chapter 37
Tuesday Nights– Buskers Night

It was around 20:00 and I was doing some building work at The Black Diamond Inn. I was thinking of how to improve Bubbles. I had a couple of quiet nights during the week. I had almost exhausted Bubbles with music.

I was laying concrete around the new extension at The Black Diamond, this part of the build was to be opened as a restaurant. I was talking to Bob Davison, who is one of the best singers in the country. Bob came up with the idea of a jazz/blues night where it could be a laid-back vibe. Bob said he would help me with this.

This was ideal because Bob was a great entertainer and would encourage people to get up and join in.

This soon turned out to be very popular. I would send food over from The Black Diamond for people to enjoy on the night, for free.

Tuesday nights: Early days, we would have a resident band, Backshift, who would play their stuff and this would give them a chance to practise new songs. The band consisted of three guys, John Cuthbert on the drums, Pete Nichol on the bass and Alan

Dickinson on the lead guitar. They played the best version of *Sultans Of Swing* by Dire Straits that I have ever heard.

To date, the buskers nights in Bubbles are still going strong and Bob is still there doing great stuff. Long may it continue!

Chapter 38
21 Strangers

On one occasion, we had booked a band called 21 Strangers. A bunch of young lads from Newcastle. I remember the night, the lads had set up their gear ready to perform and we were waiting to start at 9.00pm.

The bar was starting to fill up and these young lads went to the juke box, put in their money and all started laughing. It was them!! They had a single in the charts.

Some of the customers knew exactly who they were and started chatting to them. One of the lads in the band said to me, "He will be in later on" "Who?" I replied. "Fatty, he's coming in," a voice from the back shouted. Who they were on about was Chas Chandler, the original Bass Guitarist member of the Animals. This was the guy who introduced Jimmy Hendrix into this country from America. He was a big name and if I remember correctly, he was involved in the opening of the Metro Arena. Later on that evening, the band went down well with the crowd and lo and behold this giant of a man walked in. It was Chas Chandler.

He is no longer with us. He died in July 1996.

Hilton Valentine, another member of the Animals, lead guitarist, played with his band The Alligators.

John Steel, drummer, had also appeared with his band.

Chapter 39
Police

The police have played a part in my life.

I had never had any contact or dealings with the police, until I opened 'Bubbles'.

I made an appointment and went to see the Chief Inspector of the police, just before I opened 'Bubbles', to explain what my intentions were. His name was Mr Edd Cruddace.

I went to his office and we had a chat and I put my proposals to him.

He listened to me and replied, "Well, if you do what you say you are wanting to do, I have no problems with that. But step out of line and I will be down on you like a ton of bricks", or words to that effect.

Over the next few years, the police would show their presence in 'Bubbles', especially when we were busy, i.e. Saturday nights etc. Mr Cruddace was present most of the time. We had a good relationship as I understood my position and that of the police.

As the years went on there were a few altercations in the bar, mainly with lads who had a pint or two too many. Most of the time they had been drinking in other bars before they came into 'Bubbles'.

On one occasion there had been an incident inside 'Bubbles' and the police were called. When they arrived, I told them what had happened and pointed out the culprit. To my surprise the police said there was nothing they could do about it. I thought why?

Anyway, a few days later I saw the guy who had caused the incident. I confronted him and shall I say—we had a few words!

A couple more incidents occurred and the staff had called the police, but once again there was nothing they could do!

The trouble is, when alcohol is involved, customers seem to be invincible.

A few more incidents occurred over the years as I have mentioned some of them earlier in the book.

I have always been a law abiding person but it is a shame that I now have no respect for the police, because of the way that they have treated me. Once again, it is only the one percent.

I remember one time when I was in The Black Diamond, I was in the process of building it as it happened, when the police walked in and they embarrassingly asked if I could do them a favour. "We have come to ask if you could put your licence on the police bar in the police station, as we have not renewed our licence and we have a wedding anniversary party booked?" they asked.

"Yes, no problem," I replied.

It was quite funny, because at the time I had to go to the Magistrates Court to apply for this licence, and part of the procedure is when in the court room, the magistrates have to ask if anyone present has any objections. The police replied, "No objections."

What I have found is that a small percentage of the police have this feeling of power. Because they are the police they think that they are the law in whatever they do or say. What they seem to forget is that they are only representatives of the law. 'Servants to the public, who pay their wages'.

We need a better relationship with the police and 'Joe Public'. We are no different to each other.

Being arrested and taken to a police cell at 4.00am in the morning of a Bank Holiday Monday, then being released at around 4.00am the next morning when they knew it had been a busy day for me in the bar?…

There are a lot more incidents but it would not be the right thing for me to do, if I put more of them in.

Chapter 40
Life in the bar/Conclusion

L ife in the bar trade is not your average job. Not a 9-5 career. It's not even a job, it's a way of life. A different way of life. I have been told that there are more divorces in working the bar trade than any other profession. More heart attacks also. You have to be your own accountant, bookkeeper, solicitor, security officer and advisor to others, most of the time. When you're at work, you are on a stage where all customers can see you. You have to get on with all types of people. Some are very grateful towards you and some are downright ignorant. Some are helpful and polite whilst some are nothing but trouble. All of the time you have to deal with whatever situation you are put into to the best of your ability.

A lot of the time you have to deal with drunks. Some are violent and some are emotional. Some don't even know where they are. I have had over twenty-two years in 'Bubbles' and I can say I have had good times, but also bad. It's a shame when you can't rely on the people you should trust more than anyone.

Who I am talking about? Well… take for example, the Tax and VAT Inspectors, the Business Rates Department, the Police and also Police Barristers.

It is surprising how you can meet people by just working in a bar and become good friends with them.

I have met a lot of friends through the bar.

Have I enjoyed it? Most of the years, No.

Would I do it again? No.

Am I pleased I have done it? Yes.

I have been single, then married during this time. My two girls were born so I became a father. I also have been divorced.

I started off with nothing and I mean, nothing. I had to borrow money from breweries over the years and pay it all back. I have had to pay for everything, i.e. the decorating, utilities, stock, wages and so on. I have had people wanting to take from me in all ways.

But when I sold up in October 2007 it was just before the 2008 economic crash when the whole world went bust. No one saw it coming. All my hard work over the years was complete.

I am pleased to say that 'Bubbles' has survived the recession and is still going strong. There are four guys in there now running it as a syndicate. They are great lads and they are doing a good job of restoring the ethos of 'Bubbles' it once had in years gone by.

I would like to say I have had good times and bad during the years as a licensee. It has been downright hard work, especially the way I started both pubs from scratch. I have had good staff and bad. Most of the customers over the years have been great and I have a lot of lifelong friends from having the pubs. Only that dreaded one percent of idiots who are only out to spoil it for others and cause trouble have been the problem.

I would like to thank everyone who has frequented the pubs over the years and I hope I have managed to give them a little insight and satisfaction. The people of Ashington are genuine and what I would call 'salt of the earth'. A small working town where we are almost all the same.

A town where I grew up. A town where people would never lock their doors. People would leave money on the table for their insurance man to collect if they were not in. A town where you could go to your neighbour's house and borrow a cup of sugar if you ran out. Those days are long gone, but I do feel that there is a real comradeship with the folks of Ashington.

There has been blood, sweat and a few beers along the way.

Thank you all.